MATHS & ENGLISH FOR
CHILDCARE

Graduated exercises and practice exam

Andrew Spencer and Karen Coombes

CENGAGE
Learning

Australia • Brazil • Japan • Korea • Me:

Maths & English for Childcare

Andrew Spencer and Karen Coombes

Publishing Director: Linden Harris

Publisher: Lucy Mills

Development Editor: Claire Napoli

Editorial Assistant: Lauren Darby

Production Editor: Alison Burt

Manufacturing Buyer: Eyvett Davis

Typesetter: Cambridge Publishing
Management Limited

Cover design: HCT Creative

For product information and technology assistance, contact **emea.info@cengage.com**.

For permission to use material from this text or product, and for permission queries, email **emea.permissions@cengage.com**.

This work is adapted from *Pre Apprenticeship: Maths & Literacy Series* by Andrew Spencer published by Cengage Learning Australia Pty Limited © 2010.

British Library Cataloguing-in-Publication Data
A catalogue record for this book is available from the British Library.

ISBN: 978-1-4080-8312-3

Cengage Learning EMEA Cheriton House, North Way, Andover, Hampshire, SP10 5BE United Kingdom

Cengage Learning products are represented in Canada by Nelson Education Ltd.

For your lifelong learning solutions, visit
www.cengage.co.uk

Purchase your next print book, e-book or e-chapter at
www.cengagebrain.com

Printed in Greece by Bakis
1 2 3 4 5 6 7 8 9 10 – 15 14 13

Maths & English for Childcare

Contents

Introduction

It has always been important to understand, from a teacher's perspective, the nature of the mathematical skills students need for their future, rather than teaching them textbook mathematics. This has been a guiding principle behind the development of the content in this workbook. To teach maths that is relevant to students seeking apprenticeships is the best that we can do, to give students an education in the field that they would like to work in.

The content in this resource is aimed at the level that is needed for a student to have the best possibility of improving their maths and literacy skills specifically for trades. Students can use this workbook to prepare for an apprenticeship entry assessment, or even to assist with basic numeracy and literacy at pre-apprenticeship level. Coupled with the interactive CD, these resources have the potential to improve the students' understanding of basic maths concepts that can be applied to trades. These resources have been trialled, and they work.

Commonly used trade terms are introduced so that students have a basic understanding of terminology that they will encounter in the workplace environment. (Words that are in the glossary appear in **bold** the first time they are used.) Students who can complete this workbook and reach an 80 per cent or higher outcome in all topics will have achieved the goal of this resource. These students will go on to complete work experience, or gain an apprenticeship in the trade of their choice.

The content in this workbook is the first step towards bridging the gap between what has been learnt in previous years, and what needs to be remembered and re-learnt for use in trades. Students will significantly benefit from the consolidation of the basic maths and literacy concepts.

Every school has students who want to work with their hands, and not all students want to go to university. The best students want to learn what they do not know; and if students want to learn, this book has the potential to give them a good start in life.

This resource has been specifically tailored to prepare students for sitting apprenticeship or college admission tests, and for giving students the basic skills they will need for a career in trade. In many ways, it is a win–win situation, with students enjoying and studying relevant maths for trades and Registered Training Organisations (RTOs) receiving students that have improved basic maths and literacy skills.

All that is needed is patience, hard work, a positive attitude, a belief in yourself that you can do it and a desire to achieve. The rest is up to you.

About the authors

Andrew Spencer has studied education both within Australia and overseas. He has a Bachelor of Education, as well as a Master of Science degree in which he specialized in teacher education. Andrew has extensive experience in teaching secondary mathematics throughout New South Wales and South Australia for well over fifteen years. He has taught a range of subject areas including Maths, English, Science, Classics, Physical Education and Technical Studies. His sense of the importance of practical mathematics continued to develop with the range of subject areas he taught in.

Karen Coombes became a childcare practitioner following a career move when her own children were young. She worked in a variety of childcare settings and job roles across Greater Manchester, focusing on working with children with special educational needs. Karen achieved a Level 4 Childcare qualification and also a Masters of Education specialising in Basic Skills. She has extensive experience in teaching post-16 year-olds, and for the last 17 years she has taught a range of subject areas, including Childcare, Teaching Assistants, Health and Social Care, English, Maths and IT.

Acknowledgements

For Paula, Zach, Katelyn, Mum and Dad.
Many thanks to Mal Aubrey (GTA) and all training organisations for their input.
To the De La Salle Brothers for their selfless work with all students.
Thanks also to Dr Pauline Carter for her unwavering support for all Maths teachers.
This is for all students who value learning, who are willing to work hard and who have character …
and are characters!

For Rick, Lindsey, Samantha and Michael.
Many thanks to Darren Matthews and work colleagues for their input and support.

To all future students on their chosen career path, work hard for you never know what opportunities you may encounter whilst working in the childcare sector.

The publisher would like to thank the many copyright holders who have kindly granted us permission to reproduce material throughout this text. Every effort has been made to contact all rights holders, but in the unlikely event that anything has been overlooked, please contact the publisher directly and we will happily make the necessary arrangements at the earliest opportunity.

ENGLISH

Unit 1: Spelling

Short-answer questions

Specific instructions to students

- This is an exercise to help you to identify and correct spelling errors.
- Read the activity below, then answer accordingly.

Read the following passage and identify and correct the spelling errors.

The staff members of a chidcare centre arive at 7.00 a.m. on a Monday morning to prepare for a bussy day. The centre maneger meets with the staff at 7.10 a.m. to present the dayly rootine. The staff work through and discuss the outline of the routine. All staff members are in agrement that the minor changes that have been made by the director are good for the cognative devalopment of the children. The centre opens the doors at 7.30 a.m. and parents begin to drop off their children.

Breekfast is prepared in the kitchan and the food and drink is served to the children at their tables. Once they have finished, the children get to chooce their play activaty. Soon after the play activity, some staff members tend to the babies and change their nappyies. All staff members know of the inportance of washing their hands and they complete this task thoroughlly. Meanwhile, other staff play and exarcise with the older children. Evaryone moves inside to wash their hands and then they all guther in the main area for morning tea.

Incorrect words:

_____

_____

Correct words:

_____

_____

Short-answer questions

Specific instructions to students

- The following questions will help you practise your grammar and **punctuation**. Amend the existing text by correcting any errors that you might find.
- Read the following questions, then answer accordingly.

QUESTION 1

Which linking word or phrase could you use instead of 'whereas'?

Answer:

_____

QUESTION 2

What punctuation is missing from the following **sentence**?

> Children going into the examination needed to take with them pen pencil rubber pencil sharpener felt tips pencil crayons dictionary and an atlas

Answer:

_____
_____
_____

QUESTION 3

What is wrong with the following text? Correct the following sentence.

> Last Friday the play scheme was extremely busy; abdiya was run off her feet with all the children who had been booked in. She was pleased that she had remembered to ask zamzam to come in to help. She had felt a bit guilty as she had had to ask zamzam to travel in from manchester, where she had been on a hen night the night before

Answer:

_____
_____
_____
_____
_____

QUESTION 4

What is wrong with the following text?

> Why not visit our new after school club set in the heart of bustling Blackpool? Youre sure to receive a warm welcome, whether you want help with homework, play the latest computer games, experiment with science activities or play sport. The choice is yours! To find out more, call Natasha in 01253 4767

Answer:

_____
_____

QUESTION 5

Can you identify the mistake in this job application letter?

> Dear Madam
>
> I wish to apply for the vacancy of Level 2 **nursery** nurse at your nursery, as advertised in this week's Manchester Evening News.
>
> I have just completed my CACHE Level 2 Childcare coarse at Highfield Park College and am now looking for work in the Manchester area.
>
> I enclose a copy of my CV and look forward to hearing from you.
>
> Yours faithfully
>
> Alexia Smith

Answer:

_____

QUESTION 6

a Add the missing **full stops** and **capital letters** to this advert for a **holiday play scheme**.

> scamps, salford
>
> scamps is an established and well subscribed **holiday play scheme** they provide full day care, monday to friday, for children aged between 5 and 16 years part time places are available on request children experience a full range of activities from sport, creative activities, science experiments and trips that include cinema, ten pin bowling, Laser Quest and fun park scamps is the place for you please ring 0161 736 2701 to find out more and all about our special rates

Answer:

b Can you identify the mistake in this advert?

Answers:

_____

_____

QUESTION 7

Add **commas** to the following text to make the sense clearer.

> Using a washing machine as we know is a very simple task. Most of us have a washing machine at home yet launderettes are still popular in many locations throughout the UK. Many years ago during Victorian times doing the washing was extremely hard work and took virtually all day. In comparison to those days doing the washing is a piece of cake! Just imagine how long it would have taken in Victorian times to do the laundry that a typical nursery generates each day nowadays!

Answer:

Unit 3: Homophones

Short-answer questions

Specific instructions to students

- The following questions relate to words that sound the same but are spelt differently and have different meanings. These words are known as **homophones**.
- Read the questions carefully, then answer accordingly.

QUESTION 1

The following sentences are about two nursery nurses who have decided to go on holiday together.

a Check your knowledge of *there*, *their* and *they're* in the following sentences. Only one sentence is correct. Which one is it?

 (1) Their are too many children booked in on Friday, for the number of staff.

 (2) The manager realized that there holiday will be taken at the same time as two others.

 (3) They're going on their holiday in the early hours of Friday morning.

 (4) There going to be short staffed on Friday, as their's been too many children booked in.

Answer:

_____

b Check your knowledge of *where*, *were* and *we're* in the following sentences. Only one sentence is correct. Which one is it?

 (1) When we get to our destination, we're not sure were we'll go first?

 (2) We're sure we'll be fine, when we know where we're going.

 (3) If there's a delay, where sure that we're going to miss our connecting flight.

 (4) Once we find the hotel, were going to shower and change and go straight out.

Answer:

_____

c Check your knowledge of *too*, *to* and *two* in the following sentences. Only one sentence is correct. Which one is it?

 (1) The two of us are going on holiday to New York too.

 (2) We want to go too Staten Island too.

 (3) We're concerned that there'll be two many people on the Metro in New York.

 (4) To get too Staten Island, the two of us will need to catch the ferry.

Answer:

_____

d Check your knowledge of *buy*, *by* and *bye* in the following sentences. Only one sentence is correct. Which one is it?

 (1) We'll each have to bye a ticket to get to Staten Island by ferry.

 (2) By the way, we'll have to make sure that we buy plenty of souvenirs to take home.

 (3) Buy the time we get home, it will be a struggle to say bye to each other.

 (4) By all accounts, we'll have to bye some waterproofs for the ferry journey.

Answer:

_____

e Check your knowledge of *pause*, *paws* and *pours* in the following sentences. Only one sentence is correct. Which one is it?

 (1) If it paws down with rain, we'll go to Central Park Zoo.

 (2) If there's a pause in the rain, we'll go and see the polar bears.

 (3) It doesn't matter if their pours get wet, as they'll be swimming in their pool anyway.

 (4) Once it starts raining, though, it just paws and paws.

Answer:

_____

f Check your knowledge of *heal, he'll* and *heel* in the following sentences. Only one sentence is correct. Which one is it?

(1) While running in the rain, I slipped, fell on my knee and broke the heal of my shoe.

(2) My knee is really sore and bruised, so it will take a couple of days to heel.

(3) I'm so glad that Andrew is with me, as he'll have to lend me a bit of support.

(4) I couldn't find a cobbler, so I'll have to wait to get my heal fixed when I get home.

Answer:

_____

QUESTION 2

Check your knowledge of *there, their* and *they're* in the following sentences. Read each sentence and write the correct word in the space provided.

a The staff chose the shade of blinds to complement the colour scheme of _____ nursery.

b _____ was just enough seating in the play area.

c I wonder if I could fit another chair in the play area, over _____ ?

d I've asked the supervisor to welcome the children and a nursery nurse will hang up _____ coats for them.

e It's nearly 11.00 a.m. and _____ going to be here in a minute.

f There's a new range of dressing-up clothes in the catalogue; I've heard that _____ really good.

g I believe that the suppliers have got all of _____ costumes in stock.

QUESTION 3

Check your knowledge of *where, were* and *we're* in the following sentences. Read each sentence and write the correct word in the space provided.

a We always make sure that the children are sitting _____ they feel comfortable, ready for their story.

b _____ always making sure that all toys are clean and not broken.

c If the drinking cups aren't sterilized, _____ not prepared to use them due to the risk of cross-infection.

d When putting out the play equipment, we always have to remember _____ it is set out for health and safety reasons.

e _____ going to take the children on an outing to the park.

f We always make sure that the children put aprons on before they start painting; there would be nothing worse than if the children_____ to get paint on their clothes.

g The children _____ planting seeds in the garden.

QUESTION 4

Which of these pairs of words are NOT homophones?

(1) hear / here

(2) write / right

(3) stop / cease

(4) new / knew

Answer:

_____

QUESTION 5

The following chart relates to words that sound the same, but are spelt differently and have different meanings (homophones). Complete the chart, where applicable, providing definitions and/or a short sentence to put the word in the correct context.

Words	Definitions	Short sentence
Hear	To listen to.	
Here	In this spot.	
Weak		I felt so weak this morning, I could hardly move.
Week	A period of 7 consecutive days.	
Piece		I'll only have a small piece of chocolate cake, thank you.
Peace	Freedom from strife, arguments or war; quiet.	
Cue		During the play, he spotted his cue to speak.
Queue	To form a line while waiting.	
Allowed		
Aloud		You're not meant to speak aloud in a library.
Knew	The **past tense** of 'know'.	
New		
Stationery	Writing materials such as pens, pencils, paper and envelopes.	
Stationary		Putting the brakes on the pushchair makes it stationary.
Whole	The complete sum, amount or quantity of anything.	
Hole		My foot got wet through the hole in my shoe.
Draught	A current of air, usually of a different temperature, entering an enclosed space.	
Draft	A first version of a piece of writing, which could be subject to revision.	
Draw		
Drawer	A lidless container that slides in and out of a chest or table.	

Re-write the poster below, replacing the incorrect words with a correct homophone.

TINY PEOPLE'S NURSERY

Come and visit us in our lovely knew nursery, with ate, bright, bowled and colourful rooms. It is the perfect setting to care four you're suite little one, from berth to five years.

We offer a fun and exciting environment, every day of the weak. Weather just mourning, afternoon or full daze, you will find hour prices cheep and the service amazing!

Activities on offer include: mini mussels exercise class, 0–2 years knew multi-sensory room, 3–5 year olds are aloud in the fully supervized jungle jim. All children attending in a mourning are offered a healthy serial for breakfast.

All our childcare workers are approved by Trafford Counsel and CRB checked by lore.

You're child wood love too pay us a visit and meat some knew friends, and we will make sure there cared four, happy and protected.

Call us now on 0161-928-6000

Answer:

_____

_____

_____

_____

_____

_____

_____

_____

_____

_____

_____

_____

_____

_____

Short-answer questions

Specific instructions to students

- These are exercises to help you understand what you read.
- Read the following activities, then answer the questions that follow.

Read the following passage and answer the questions in sentence form.

Lisa, the nursery manager, scheduled bed and rest time for all children at around 12.15 p.m., ensuring that all children rested according to their individual needs. Once most of the children were asleep, the staff cleaned up the lunch plates, dishes and cups and began preparing for the afternoon craft activities. Sue took out the paints and brushes and checked that everything was clean, safe and in good order for the painting activity. Daniel gathered the paper scissors, cleaned them and checked them to make sure that they were in a safe working condition. Anthony organized four different sets of coloured paper for another craft activity.

Soon Libby heard the babies waking up and she asked Jeremy to check on them. Jeremy returned and said that most of the babies were now awake and Libby agreed that it was OK to open the main door to the room. Libby and Jeremy worked well together as a team to change the babies' nappies and to give each one a toy to play with.

All of the children were working quietly on their craft activity when, all of a sudden, everyone heard a fire engine siren! Excitement in the centre reached a peak when Michael the fireman entered the nursery at 2.00 p.m. Michael belongs to the local fire brigade and he visits many childcare settings to talk with the children about fire safety. Everyone gathered in the main area and Michael talked about the importance of fire safety for people of all ages. The babies needed a well-earned rest after all of the excitement. They had their nappies changed and were put down for a sleep at around 3.00 p.m.

QUESTION 1

What time did Lisa schedule bed and rest time for?

Answer:

QUESTION 2

What task did the staff undertake once the children were asleep?

Answer:

QUESTION 3

In what ways did Libby and Jeremy work well together as a team?

Answer:

QUESTION 4

What caused the 'excitement' in the nursery in the afternoon?

Answer:

QUESTION 5

At what time did the babies need a well-earned rest in the afternoon and what task was completed before they went for their sleep?

Answer:

Read the following passage and answer the questions in sentence form.

Ellis was an apprentice nursery nurse and fairly new to his role. He liked to get into work early at 7.30 a.m., and this morning was no exception, even though the first child was not expected to arrive until 8.00 a.m.

His supervisor, Jade, had left him a list of jobs that needed to be done, but he was not sure whether any of these required immediate attention, or if they were of equal importance. Jade liked him to keep occupied while he was not busy helping out other colleagues in the nursery. He checked with his supervisor to find out which jobs needed doing first, then prioritised the jobs and ticked them off as he carried them out. Jade was busy for most of the day interviewing for a new nursery nurse to join the team.

While Ellis was carrying out these jobs, he was asked by his colleagues to carry out some other duties. Emma, the **pre-school** room supervisor, asked him to prepare seven glue pots and spreaders ready for the children. He also tidied up after the creative activity with the children, before Emma left to go to a dental appointment. Ellis managed to take a 15-minute break between helping Emma with the children and preparing the children's drinks for lunchtime.

He found that ticking off jobs as he completed them was really helpful, as he had to keep stopping so he could attend to requests from colleagues. Molly, another nursery nurse, wanted him to stock up the disposable nappies and wipes in the baby room. Molly asked Ellis to help her changing the babies' nappies.

Later on in the afternoon, Ellis also helped out on reception, as the receptionist had gone home sick at 2.00 p.m. He welcomed parents and visitors to the nursery, ensuring that visitors signed in and were given ID badges to wear. He answered the telephone and updated children's records on the computer. It was lucky that he had managed to eat his lunch between 1.00 and 1.30 p.m.; otherwise it would have been difficult to take a break.

As the last few children were collected from the nursery, Ellis managed a quick break of 10 minutes. When he returned, he tidied the play area and helped wash the used paint pots and brushes. He then set up the free play area ready for the following day. It had been a long day, but he had enjoyed the variety of jobs that the day had brought. All the staff finished work at the nursery at 6.00 p.m. and left to go home.

QUESTION 1

What did Emma ask Ellis to do for her?

Answer:

QUESTION 2

How did Ellis help Molly?

Answer:

QUESTION 3

Ellis started work at 7.30 a.m. and he finished at 6.00 p.m.; how much time did he take for breaks and lunch?

Answer:

QUESTION 4

What was the supervisor occupied with for the majority of the day?

Answer:

QUESTION 5

What did Ellis make visitors to the nursery do?

Answer:

QUESTION 6

What evidence is there of Ellis planning and managing his workload?

Answer:

Short-answer questions

Specific instructions to students

- The following questions relate to writing letters and emails.
- Read the question carefully, then answer accordingly.

QUESTION 1

Which type of letter is likely to be **informal** in style?

(1) Making an appointment to see the bank manager

(2) Confirming an interview date

(3) Email to a friend

(4) Making a complaint

Answer:

_____

QUESTION 2

As well as thinking about the recipient of your letter or email, what else do you need to think about when writing a letter or email?

(1) The content

(2) The style

(3) The layout

(4) All of the above

Answer:

_____

QUESTION 3

True or false? When writing an email, you need to select the email address of the person you want to receive it before selecting the 'send' button.

Answer:

_____

QUESTION 4

How would you describe the 'content' of a letter or email?

(1) The formality with which you are writing

(2) The ideas and information you are writing

(3) The amount of text you are writing

Answer:

_____

QUESTION 5

When sending an email, if you want other people to receive it but do not want to share their email addresses, which box would you select?

(1) 'Forward'   (3) 'Bcc'

(2) 'Cc'   (4) 'Send / Receive'

Answer:

_____

QUESTION 6

Parts **a** to **h** relate to the letter of complaint below. Please read it carefully and refer to it to answer the questions.

a What is wrong with the closing phrase at the end of the letter?

Answer:

_____

_____

b What does the word 'inconvenience' mean, in line 23?

Answer:

_____

c Which **paragraph** of the letter outlines the reason for the complaint?

Answer:

_____

Kiddies People
22 Slinger Road
Hale
Cheshire
WA13 1BN

5

15 April 2013

The Manager
Tom Bob's Play Equipment
Nursery Avenue
10 Blackpool
Lancashire
FY5 9ER

Dear Sir or Madam

Your office contacted me on 27 March regarding the urgent repairs that were required to my wooden
15 climbing frame, as the model AXCH 125 had been identified as representing a safety hazard. Your company service engineer carried out the necessary repairs on 1 April.

Within a day I noticed that the rope bridge was not working correctly, as a child fell from the equipment when the supporting pole moved and twisted. I have had to offer the parents a reduction in fees, as compensation for this distressing experience. I have also had to close of part of our outdoor play area, as I
20 cannot run the risk of using this piece of equipment.

I rely heavily on the use of this piece of equipment and the loss of it has caused me great inconvenience and upset to the children. As none of this is my fault, I am appealing to you to replace the equipment and to reimburse me for the loss of earnings which I have incurred through the child's accident.

I hope to hear from you in the near future.

25 Yours sincerely

Mary Jolly

d Line 19 contains a spelling error. What is the word and how should it be spelt?

Answer:

_____

e Which word or phrase, used in the letter, means 'to pay me back'?

Answer:

_____

f What is the main complaint in this letter?

Answer:

_____

g How would you describe the style of writing used by Mary in her letter?

Answer:

_____

h In which paragraph does she use her most persuasive language?

Answer:

_____

QUESTION 7

The following exercises contain a mixture of words that have either already been shortened, using **apostrophes**, or require shortening. Read them carefully, and then reword the sentences accordingly.

a They've just spotted that they'll have to order more paint before next week otherwise they will run out.

Answer:

_____

_____

b I'd love to own my own nursery, but I'll have to get more experience before I consider doing so.

Answer:

_____

_____

c It is only 10.30 a.m. and I cannot believe how hungry I am!

Answer:

_____

d He won't believe that I missed the last bus home.

Answer:

_____

e She doesn't like to be absent from work as it puts too much pressure on the others.

Answer:

_____

_____

QUESTION 8

If you are applying for a job, what do you not need to include?

(1) What qualifications and experience you have

(2) Your plans for the future

(3) How long it will take to commute

(4) Why you want to work for the company

Answer:

QUESTION 9

Ellie has written in response to the advertisement that she spotted in her local newspaper, shown below.

> Nursery nurse required for local nursery.
> Must have 2 years' experience.
> Please send your CV and covering letter, to:
> Lynn Cheetham
> Little Treasures
> Claremont Road
> Manchester

She has asked you to look over her covering letter to see if she has included all the relevant points, before she posts it. She has also asked if you can help her write it again, if necessary.

> Hi there
>
> I want the job you've put in the local newspaper this week. I've been in childcare for 2 years and I can get people to vouch for me, if you want. Here's a list of my qualifications and where I've worked before, in with this letter.
>
> You can call me on 07863 03694
>
> Ellie

In the blue box below, using 200 words, help Ellie by rewriting the short covering letter to accompany her CV, including the correct structure, content and layout for a **formal** letter. Consider formal qualifications and personal skills. Include any experience such as work placement or voluntary work.

Answer:

Short-answer questions

Specific instructions to students

- The following questions will help you understand how to work with and interpret data.
- Read the following questions, then answer accordingly.

The following questions relate to a primary school called Elmtree. It is set in a busy town location where children enjoy a full range of lessons.

QUESTION 1

Elmtree has included this diagram in their staff handbook, to show the staff structure. The next few questions are related to this diagram.

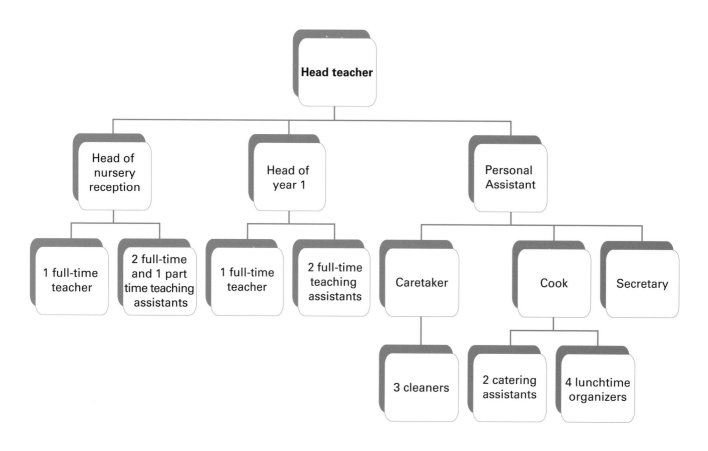

a What is this type of diagram called?

Answer:

_____

b How many members of staff is the Personal Assistant responsible for?

Answer:

_____

c How many members of staff report directly to the head teacher?

Answer:

_____

d How many members of staff, including the Head teacher, work at Elmtree?

Answer:

_____

QUESTION 2

The next few questions relate to the holiday entitlements and attendance bonus scheme, provided below, as they appear in the staff handbook at Elmtree.

Number of years in service	Annual holiday entitlement	❖ Additional holiday for 100% attendance
Less than 1 year	10 days (pro rata)	N/A
1–3 years	15 days	0.5 day
4–6 years	20 days	1 day
7–9 years	25 days	1.5 days
Over 10 years	30 days	2 days

❖ *This additional holiday bonus is only applied in the year following a 100% attendance record.*

a How have the details of the holiday entitlement been presented?

Answer:

_____

b What is the maximum annual holiday entitlement at Elmtree, without taking any available additional holiday bonus into account?

Answer:

_____

c If a member of staff has worked at Elmtree for 8 years, how many days holiday are they entitled to?

Answer:

_____

d True or false? The holiday entitlements table provided contains 3 rows and 5 columns.

Answer:

_____

e How much additional time off would a member of staff receive if they had a 100% attendance record in the previous year and had worked for Elmtree for 11 years?

Answer:

_____

f If a member of staff had a total holiday entitlement of 20 days and 1 day attendance bonus, how long would they have worked at Elmtree?

Answer:

_____

g What would the total holiday entitlement, including attendance bonus, for a member of staff who had 100% attendance record in their previous year and had worked at Elmtree for 8 years?

Answer:

_____

QUESTION 3

The next few questions relate to the staff handbook that all new members of staff at Elmtree receive upon starting their employment.

a The staff handbook is designed to do which of the following?

(1) Persuade

(2) Advise

(3) Instruct

(4) Convince

Answer:

_____

b The first page of the staff handbook contains a welcome message from the manager. How would this message be most likely to be presented?

(1) In memo format

(2) In charts and graphs

(3) In paragraphs

(4) In bullet points

Answer:

_____

c The staff handbook contains information about actions to take in the case of emergencies, such as discovering a fire in the workplace. This information would be best presented in which of the following forms?

(1) Flow chart

(2) Pie chart

(3) Table

(4) Line graph

Answer:

d Assuming that all new employees receive basic training on how to tackle small fires in the workplace, how would it be best to illustrate the use of firefighting equipment in the staff handbook?

(1) Using signs

(2) Using diagrams

(3) Using bar charts

(4) Using tables

Answer:

Speaking and Listening – Planning a Fundraising Event

SCENARIO 1

You are working in a nursery and need to have a meeting with some of your co-workers to discuss a fundraising event. You will have to consider when and where this event will take place, what the theme might be and what will be needed on the day.

Tasks will need to be allocated to each person and costs will need to be considered, including price per person to attend the event. You are also required to persuade a senior manager to allow holding the event.

Chairperson
Your role is to lead and control the meeting. You must manage time, facilitate the discussion, mediate any disagreement and summarize agreements. You need to agree the date and set tasks for members in the group.

Samantha
Your role is to research themes for parties and consider what will be needed for that theme. You need to make the best decision in consultation with others in the group.

Ghislaine
Your role is to carry out research into the food and drinks that will be needed for the celebration. You need to make the best decision in consultation with others in the group.

Josh
Your role is to research venues for the event. You will need to make the best decision in consultation with others in the group.

Leanne
Your role is to carry out research involving prices people would be willing to pay / what other events normally charge. You will need to make the best decision in consultation with others in the group.

SCENARIO 2

You are organizing a fundraising event. The head teacher has asked you and some colleagues to plan money-raising activities for all ticket holders on the night as she feels this will make the event more exciting.

Chairperson

Your role is to lead and control the meeting. You must manage time, facilitate the discussion, mediate any disagreement and summarize agreements. You need to set tasks to members in the group.

Alfie

Your role is to carry out research into raffle activities. You need to share and discuss your ideas with others in the group.

Linzi

Your role is to carry out research into quiz activities. You need to share your ideas and discuss your ideas with others in the group.

Amina

Your role is to carry out research into karaoke activities. You need to share your ideas and discuss your ideas with others in the group.

Whitney

Your role is to carry out research into general fundraising activities/ideas. You need to share your ideas and discuss your ideas with others in the group.

MATHEMATICS

It is important to show your working to indicate how you calculated your answer. Use this workbook to practise the questions and record your answers. Use the blank Notes pages at the back of the book to record your working.

Unit 7: General Mathematics

Short-answer questions

Specific instructions to students

- This unit will help you to improve your general mathematical skills.
- Read the following questions and answer all of them in the spaces provided.
- You need to show all working, you can use the blank Notes pages at the back of this book.

QUESTION 1

What unit of measurement would you use to measure:

a The **area** of an outdoor play area?

Answer:

_____

b The temperature of an oven?

Answer:

_____

c The amount of hand sanitizer?

Answer:

_____

d The weight of a one-year-old baby?

Answer:

_____

e The energy in a light bulb?

Answer:

_____

f The length of a pair of scissors?

Answer:

_____

g The cost of an educational book?

Answer:

_____

QUESTION 2

Write an example of the following and give an instance where it may be found in the childcare sector:

a Percentages

Answer:

---

b Decimals

Answer:

---

c Fractions

Answer:

---

d Mixed numbers

Answer:

---

e Ratios

Answer:

---

f Angles

Answer:

QUESTION 3

Convert the following units:

a 12 kg to grams

Answer:

---

b 4 tonnes to kilograms

Answer:

---

c 120 cm to metres

Answer:

---

d 1140 ml to litres

Answer:

---

e 1650 g to kilograms

Answer:

---

f 1880 kg to tonnes

Answer:

---

g 13 m to centimetres

Answer:

---

h 4.5 litres to millilitres

Answer:

QUESTION 4

Write the following in descending order:

0.4   0.04   4.1   40.0   400.00   4.0

Answer:

QUESTION 5

Write the **decimal** number that is halfway between the following:

a 0.2 and 0.4

Answer:

---

b 1.8 and 1.9

Answer:

---

c 12.4 and 12.5

Answer:

---

d 28.3 and 28.4

Answer:

---

e 101.5 and 101.7

Answer:

QUESTION 6

Round off the following numbers to two decimal places:

a   12.346

Answer:

b   2.251

Answer:

c   123.897

Answer:

d   688.882

Answer:

e   1209.741

Answer:

QUESTION 7

Estimate the following by approximation:

a $1288 \times 19 =$

Answer:

b $201 \times 20 =$

Answer:

c $497 \times 12.2 =$

Answer:

d $1008 \times 10.3 =$

Answer:

e $399 \times 22 =$

Answer:

f $201 - 19 =$

Answer:

g $502 - 61 =$

Answer:

h $1003 - 49 =$

Answer:

i $10\ 001 - 199 =$

Answer:

j $99.99 - 39.8 =$

Answer:

QUESTION 8

What do the following add up to?

a   £4, £4.99 and £144.95

Answer:

b   8.75, 6.9 and 12.55

Answer:

c   65 ml, 18 ml and 209 ml

Answer:

d   21.3 g, 119 g and 884.65 g

Answer:

QUESTION 9

Subtract the following:

a   2338 from 7117

Answer:

b 1786 from 3112

Answer:

_____

c 5979 from 8014

Answer:

_____

d 11 989 from 26 221

Answer:

_____

e 108 767 from 231 111

Answer:

_____

QUESTION 10

Use division to solve the following:

a $2177 \div 7 =$

Answer:

_____

b $4484 \div 4 =$

Answer:

_____

c $63.9 \div 0.3 =$

Answer:

_____

d $121.63 \div 1.2 =$

Answer:

_____

e $466.88 \div 0.8 =$

Answer:

_____

The following information is provided for Question 11.

To solve using BODMAS, in order from left to right solve the Brackets first, then Order ('to the power of') then Division, then Multiplication, then Addition and lastly Subtraction. The following example has been done for your reference.

EXAMPLE :

Solve $(4 \times 7) \times 2 + 6 - 4$.

STEP 1

Solve the Brackets first: $(4 \times 7) = 28$

STEP 2

No Division so next solve Multiplication: $28 \times 2 = 56$

STEP 3

Addition is next: $56 + 6 = 62$

STEP 4

Subtraction is the last process: $62 - 4 = 58$

FINAL ANSWER

58

QUESTION 11

Using BODMAS, solve:

a $(6 \times 9) \times 5 + 7 - 2 =$

Answer:

_____

b $(9 \times 8) \times 4 + 6 - 1 =$

Answer:

_____

c $3 \times (5 \times 7) + 11 - 8 =$

Answer:

_____

d $5 \times (8 \times 3) + 9 - 6 =$

Answer:

_____

e $7 + 6 \times 3 + (9 \times 6) - 9 =$

Answer:

_____

f $6 + 9 \times 4 + (6 \times 7) - 21 =$

Answer:

_____

Unit 8: Basic Operations

Section A: Addition L1

Short-answer questions

Specific instructions to students

- This section will help you to improve your addition skills for basic operations.
- Read the questions below and answer all of them in the spaces provided.
- You need to show all working, you can use the blank Notes pages at the back of this book.

QUESTION 1

A supervisor purchases items for a **playgroup** which includes four small chairs for a total of £125, storage bins for £60 and some bottles of hand sanitizer for £35. What is the total?

Answer:

QUESTION 2

Four computers costing a total of £3980 are purchased for a childcare centre, as well as two printers for £130. How much, in total, has been spent?

Answer:

QUESTION 3

A pre-school centre stocks 57 plates, 68 cups and 123 pairs of disposable gloves. How many items, in total, are in stock?

Answer:

QUESTION 4

An **after-school club** buys four bottles of hand sanitizer for a total of £48, three learning charts together for £51, five dance CDs in a box set for £95 and two new disposable cameras together for £34. How much in total has been spent?

Answer:

QUESTION 5

Family day care uses the following amounts of juice in one day: 1500 ml in the morning, 1400 ml for lunch and 2000 ml in the afternoon. What amount has been used in total?

Answer:

QUESTION 6

Six books based on nursery rhymes are purchased for a **parent and toddler group** at the following costs: £8, £12, £19, £5, £6 and £9. How much has been spent in total?

Answer:

QUESTION 7

A number of first-aid kits need restocking, so the following items are purchased: plasters for £13, gauze dressings for £12 and saline solution for £9. What is the total cost of the items?

Answer:

QUESTION 8

Eight bottles of sun cream are purchased for a total of £55, seven containers of wipes together for £49 and three packets of toilet rolls on special offer for £24. How much has been spent?

Answer:

QUESTION 9

A holiday play scheme purchases pencils, paper, crayons and paint costing £29. Twelve sun hats are also purchased for £144 and learning toys are purchased for £120. What is the total?

Answer:

QUESTION 10

The childcare fees after a rebate are £189, £252 and £315 for three different children. How much does the total come to?

Answer:

Section B: Subtraction ⒧

Short-answer questions

Specific instructions to students

- This section will help you to improve your subtraction skills for basic operations.
- Read the following questions and answer all of them in the spaces provided.
- You need to show all working, you can use the blank Notes pages at the back of this book.

QUESTION 1

If there are 125 nappies in stock and 19 are used in one day, how many remain in stock?

Answer:

_____

QUESTION 2

There are 70 bed sheets in stock at a childcare centre. If 13 are soiled and need cleaning, how many remain?

Answer:

_____

QUESTION 3

A childcare centre spends £1113 in one month on indoor and outdoor equipment. If £2000 is budgeted for equipment, how much money is left?

Answer:

_____

QUESTION 4

A family **day care centre** uses 39 paint pots over a month from a box that contained 160. How many are left?

Answer:

_____

QUESTION 5

A gym set costs £2995 at a department store. The gym set is on sale and the store takes off a discount of £199.00. How much needs to be paid?

Answer:

_____

QUESTION 6

Over the course of a week, a centre uses 16 paint brushes from a box containing 50 paint brushes. How many are left in the box?

Answer:

QUESTION 7

A holiday play scheme uses the following amounts of paper for craft activities over a month: 55 sheets in week one, 38 sheets in week two, 69 sheets in week three, and 147 sheets in week four. If one ream of paper contains 500 sheets, how many sheets remain in the ream?

Answer:

QUESTION 8

Seventy-four children attend an after-school club. If a total of 93 were originally booked in, how many did not attend?

Answer:

QUESTION 9

The children are put down for a sleep at 11.45 a.m. If they wake at 12.30 p.m., how long have they slept for?

Answer:

QUESTION 10

Six two-litre containers of juice are refrigerated in the morning. By the afternoon, 500 ml remains. How much in litres and millilitres has been consumed?

Answer:

Section C: Multiplication 🄛

Short-answer questions

Specific instructions to students

- This section will help you to improve your multiplication skills for basic operations.
- Read the following questions and answer all of them in the spaces provided.
- You need to show all working, you can use the blank Notes pages at the back of this book.

QUESTION 1

If one two-litre container of juice costs £3, how much would nine two-litre containers cost?

Answer:

QUESTION 2

If pots of paint cost £8 each, how much would 24 pots of paint cost?

Answer:

QUESTION 3

A face painter charges £4 per child at a holiday play scheme activity day. If 36 children wanted face painting, what would be the total cost?

Answer:

QUESTION 4

A centre purchases window blinds that cost £239 each. What would be the total cost for four window blinds?

Answer:

QUESTION 5

Six new mattresses are purchased for the babies' room at a cost of £33 each. What would be the total cost?

Answer:

QUESTION 6

A holiday play scheme charges £11 per person for an excursion to a cinema. If 55 children attended the excursion, what would be the total cost?

Answer:

QUESTION 7

On average, an after-school club uses 9 l of hand sanitizer each month. How much sanitizer is used over 18 months?

Answer:

QUESTION 8

If a **childminder** uses 17 pairs of disposable gloves per week, how many would be used over a year?

Answer:

QUESTION 9

If a playgroup uses 21 nappies per day on average, how many would be needed over a 30-day month?

Answer:

QUESTION 10

Thirteen loaves of bread are used by the cook to make sandwiches for the children each week. How many loaves would be used over four weeks?

Answer:

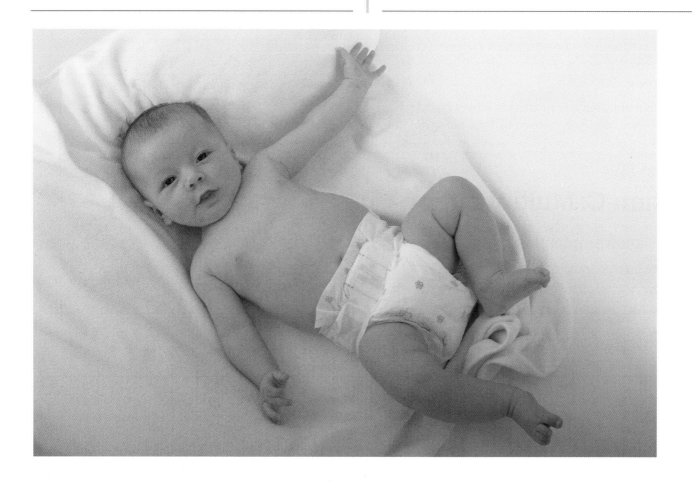

Section D: Division L1

Short-answer questions

Specific instructions to students

- This section will help you to improve your division skills for basic operations.
- Read the following questions and answer all of them in the spaces provided.
- You need to show all working, you can use the blank Notes pages at the back of this book.

QUESTION 1

A holiday play scheme has 24 children booked in for a Friday. If there are six tables, how many children could be allocated to each table?

Answer:

QUESTION 2

If a childcare worker earns £675 (before tax) for working a five-day week, how much would they earn per day?

Answer:

QUESTION 3

An after-school club buys 210 bottles of sun cream in bulk. Each box contains 30 bottles. How many boxes are there?

Answer:

QUESTION 4

A craft box contains 72 coloured pencils which are distributed equally to 12 children. How many coloured pencils will each child receive?

Answer:

QUESTION 5

Six containers of waterproof felt pens cost £33. How much is this per container?

Answer:

QUESTION 6

Over a month, an after-school club needs to replace 16 paint brushes. How many need replacing, on average, per week?

Answer:

QUESTION 7

At an end-of-financial-year audit, a worker counts 72 nappies in stock. If the nappies are packed so that there are six in each bag, how many bags are there?

Answer:

QUESTION 8

Forty-eight glue sticks are ordered for a holiday play scheme. If there are four in each packet, how many packets are there?

Answer:

QUESTION 9

During a holiday play scheme, an excursion to the cinema has been organized. If there are 120 people, including children and staff, and each bus holds 40 people, how many buses need to be ordered?

Answer:

QUESTION 10

An after-school club facility has 20 l of water in containers for 40 children. How many 250 ml cups of water have been catered for each child?

Answer:

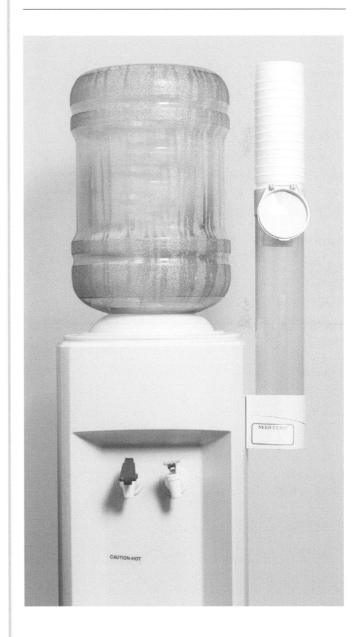

Section A: Addition (L1)

QUESTION 1

Four new storage bins for the playroom are purchased for £32.60. Name tags are also purchased to stick on the front of the bins at a cost of £4.50. How much is spent in total?

Answer:

QUESTION 2

A centre manager buys a set of paint brushes for £39.95, four pairs of scissors for £24.95, six reams of paper for £44.55 and some sticky tape for £9.50. How much is spent?

Answer:

QUESTION 3

The fees for two days of part-time childcare are £62.50 and £31.25. How much is this in total?

Answer:

QUESTION 4

An invoice for food for a family childcare setting includes fruit for £15.50, juice for £18.75 and bread for £8.50. What is the total?

Answer:

QUESTION 5

Purchases for an after-school care programme include magazines costing £28.99, sports equipment for £106.50, hand sanitizer for £12.30 and aprons for £35.90. What is the total?

Answer:

QUESTION 6

An employee travels 35.8 km, 36.5 km, 32.7 km and 39.9 km for work-related tasks for a childcare centre. How far is travelled in total?

Answer:

QUESTION 7

The cost for the bus per person to visit a science and technology exhibition, as part of an excursion by a holiday play scheme, is £5.50. Admittance to the exhibition is £3.75 per person. What will be the total cost per person?

Answer:

QUESTION 8

Three children purchase ice creams at a community centre for £13.50, as well as three bags of lollies for £4.50. What is the total cost?

Answer:

QUESTION 9

A family day care centre purchases soap costing £14.80, toilet paper costing £13.65 and hand towels costing £26.45. How much is spent in total?

Answer:

QUESTION 10

If a child had arrived at a nursery at 9.15 a.m. and had a nap at 11.30 a.m., how long had the child been at the nursery before having the nap?

Answer:

Section B: Subtraction 🔳

Short-answer questions

Specific instructions to students

- This section will help you to improve your subtraction skills when working with decimals.
- Read the following questions and answer all of them in the spaces provided.
- You need to show all working, you can use the blank Notes pages at the back of this book.

QUESTION 1

An invoice for play equipment totals £338.80. The manager pays for it out of petty cash which has £417.35 in the account. How much is left in petty cash?

Answer:

QUESTION 2

A holiday play scheme worker gets paid £468.50 for a week's work. If £118.55 is used to pay the bills, £55.75 for petrol and £76.90 for entertainment, how much is left?

Answer:

QUESTION 3

An after-school club purchases art-and-craft materials for £189.50 and a discount of £25.00 is given by the art shop. How much is the final cost?

Answer:

QUESTION 4

A childcare worker works 38 hours and earns £445.60. The worker uses £48.85 for petrol and £38.75 for going out. How much is left?

Answer:

QUESTION 5

Eleven story books are purchased for a family day care centre along with three posters on water safety. The total comes to £137.50. The bill is paid with three £50 notes. How much change is given?

Answer:

QUESTION 6

If dressing-up costumes cost £82.50 and are paid for with two £50 notes, how much change is given?

Answer:

QUESTION 7

Seven rhyme books are purchased for an after-school club. The total comes to £63.50. What change is given if four £20 notes are used to pay the bill?

Answer:

QUESTON 8

Eight 750 ml containers of sun cream are purchased to take on an excursion to the beach. If each container cost £8.50 and they were paid for with three £20 notes and one £10 note, how much change should be received?

Answer:

QUESTION 9

Six new tricycles are purchased for £326.50. If eight £50 notes are used to pay the bill, how much change is given?

Answer:

QUESTION 10

A holiday play scheme purchases the following resources: science experiment equipment for £68.50, a set of Zumba dance CDs for £99.50 and 10 plastic dinosaurs for £19.50. If petty cash has £876.50 in it before the purchases, how much will be in petty cash after the purchases?

Answer:

Section C: Multiplication

Short-answer questions

Specific instructions to students

- This section will help you to improve your multiplication skills when working with decimals.
- Read the following questions and answer all of them in the spaces provided.
- You need to show all working, you can use the blank Notes pages at the back of this book.

QUESTION 1

If a large colouring book based on saving the environment costs £9.95, how much will five cost for the toddlers' room?

Answer:

QUESTION 2

Six containers of hand wipes are used on average each week at day care. How many containers are used in one year?

Answer:

QUESTION 3

A family day care centre replaces seven water bottles at a cost of £4.50 each. What is the total?

Answer:

QUESTION 4

If a nursery purchases eight rolls of crêpe paper for £3.75 each, how much is the total cost?

Answer:

QUESTION 5

A manager of an after-school club purchases nine sets of number blocks for £19.95 each. What is the total?

Answer:

QUESTION 6

A childcare worker earns £15.50 per hour. If the worker works 38 hours in a week, how much is earned?

Answer:

QUESTION 7

Eight air conditioners costing £682.50 each are purchased for eight childcare centres. How much has been spent?

Answer:

QUESTION 8

A nursery purchases educational CDs based on numeracy and literacy for their computers that cost £19.85 each. If 13 more of the same CDs are purchased the following year, how much will the invoice be?

Answer:

QUESTION 9

A manager purchases three computer workstations for the nursery at a cost of £355.00 each. How much is the total outlay?

Answer:

QUESTION 10

A holiday play scheme worker earns £130.65 per day before tax. How much is earned for a five-day week?

Answer:

Section D: Division Ⓛ1 Ⓛ2

Short-answer questions

Specific instructions to students

- This section will help you to improve your division skills when working with decimals.
- Read the following questions and answer all of them in the spaces provided.
- You need to show all working, you can use the blank Notes pages at the back of this book.

QUESTION 1

An assistant manager earns £628.55 for a six-day working week. How much is earned for each day?

Answer:

QUESTION 2

Five musical instruments are purchased for a total of £82.50. How much does each musical instrument cost?

Answer:

QUESTION 3

Nine packets of pipe cleaners cost £31.50. How much does each packet cost?

Answer:

QUESTION 4

Four packets of glitter pens are purchased for an after-school club at a cost of £22. How much is this per packet?

Answer:

QUESTION 5

Forty children attend a performance of cultural dancing. The total cost comes to £260. How much is the cost per child?

Answer:

QUESTION 6

A childcare worker wants to teach a unit on 'birds, bats, butterflies and frogs'. The resource materials cost £52 in total. If six children are being taught the unit, how much does this work out to per child?

Answer:

QUESTION 7

Eight packets of ice blocks are purchased for £70 as part of a science experiment with the theme 'water, ice and steam'. How much does each packet of ice blocks cost?

Answer:

QUESTION 8

A live reptile show is hired for a holiday play scheme at a cost of £166.25. If 35 children attend the show, how much is the cost per child??

Answer:

QUESTION 9

Eight puzzles based on environmental issues are purchased by a setting at a cost of £124. How much is the cost per puzzle?

Answer:

QUESTION 10

Triplets purchase three of the same dressing-up costumes for a total of £77.25. What is the cost of each costume?

Answer:

Unit 10: Fractions

Section A: Addition

QUESTION 1

$\frac{1}{2} + \frac{4}{5} =$

Answer:

_____

QUESTION 2

$2\frac{2}{4} + 1\frac{2}{3} =$

Answer:

_____

QUESTION 3

Two red-colour paint pots used for face painting are $\frac{1}{4}$ full and $\frac{1}{2}$ full respectively. How much red colour is remaining as a fraction of one pot?

Answer:

_____

QUESTION 4

Four bottles of sun cream are $\frac{1}{3}$ full. How many bottles of sun cream, as a fraction, are there in total?

Answer:

_____

QUESTION 5

Two water bottles are $\frac{2}{3}$ full and $\frac{1}{4}$ full prior to a science experiment about the water cycle. How much water is there, in total, as a fraction of one bottle?

Answer:

_____

Section B: Subtraction

QUESTION 1

$\frac{2}{3} - \frac{1}{4} =$

Answer:

_____

QUESTION 2

$2\frac{2}{3} - 1\frac{1}{4} =$

Answer:

_____

QUESTION 3

A bottle of glue is $\frac{2}{3}$ full. If $\frac{1}{3}$ is used on an art activity, how much is left as a fraction?

Answer:

_____

QUESTION 4

Prior to an excursion, a family day care worker has $2\frac{1}{2}$ containers of sun cream. If $1\frac{1}{3}$ is used on the excursion, how many containers of sun cream are left, as a fraction?

Answer:

_____

QUESTION 5

An after-school club has $2\frac{3}{4}$ bottles of hand sanitizer in the toilets. If $1\frac{1}{2}$ bottles are used over two weeks, how many bottles are left in total, as a fraction?

Answer:

_____

Section C: Multiplication

Short-answer questions

Specific instructions to students

- This section is designed to help you to improve your multiplication skills when working with fractions.
- Read the following questions and answer all of them in the spaces provided.
- You need to show all working, you can use the blank Notes pages at the back of this book.

QUESTION 1

$\frac{2}{4} \times \frac{2}{3} =$

Answer:

_____

QUESTION 2

$2\frac{2}{3} \times 1\frac{1}{2} =$

Answer:

_____

QUESTION 3

A group of children on an excursion use two bottles of sun cream that were $\frac{2}{3}$ full to begin with. What is the total number of bottles of sun cream used, as a fraction?

Answer:

_____

QUESTION 4

A child uses up three tubes of paint that were $\frac{3}{4}$ full at the beginning of an art activity. How many tubes have been used, as a fraction?

Answer:

_____

QUESTION 5

A childcare worker uses four small bottles of glue that were each $\frac{1}{3}$ full to make dinosaur figures for an art activity. How many bottles are used, as a fraction?

Answer:

_____

Section D: Division ⓛ ⓛ₂

QUESTION 1

$\frac{2}{3} \div \frac{1}{4} =$

Answer:

QUESTION 2

$2\frac{3}{4} \div 1\frac{1}{3} =$

Answer:

QUESTION 3

Three storage containers are full of toys for the children. The room supervisor decides to split all of the toys into four storage containers. As a fraction, how full will each of the four containers be?

Answer:

QUESTION 4

During a trip to a national park, three children forgot to bring their water bottles. The assistant supervisor had 2 litres of water (equivalent to 2000 millilitres) and three empty water bottles. As a fraction of a litre, how much water could be evenly poured into the three empty bottles?

Answer:

QUESTION 5

Paint is to be diluted for a special art activity. The room leader had two bottles of blue paint and divided it evenly between six empty paint pallets. As a fraction, how much will be poured into each of the six empty paint pallets from the two full colour bottles?

Answer:

Unit 11: Percentages

Short-answer questions

Specific instructions to students

- In this unit, you will be able to practise and improve your skills in working out **percentages** and **ratios**.
- Read the following questions and answer all of them in the spaces provided.
- You need to show all working, you can use the blank Notes pages at the back of this book.

10% rule: Move the decimal one place to the left to get 10%.

EXAMPLE

10% of £45.00 would be £4.50

QUESTION 1

The bill for a holiday play scheme for two brothers comes to £220.00. The parent works for the local council and has a voucher for a 10% discount.

a   How much will the discount be?

Answer:

_____

b   What will the bill come to after the 10% is taken off?

Answer:

_____

QUESTION 2

Three new scooters are purchased for £175.00 for the outdoor play area. A '10% off' voucher is used to reduce the final cost.

a   How much will the discount be?

Answer:

_____

b   What is the cost of the final bill?

Answer:

_____

QUESTION 3

Air conditioners are purchased for the babies' room and the toddlers' room at a total cost of £1198.50. The centre was given a 10% discount by a business that supports childcare.

a   How much will the discount be?

Answer:

_____

b   What is the final cost?

Answer:

_____

QUESTION 4

A childcare centre manager buys five music CDs for £124.80. A 5% discount is given.

a   How much is the discount worth?

Answer:

_____

b   What is the final total? (Hint: find 10%, halve it, then subtract it from the final price.)

Answer:

_____

QUESTION 5

The cook purchases the following items for morning break: juice for £20, fruit for £69 and milk for £13.

a   How much is the total?

Answer:

_____

b   How much would a 20% discount be?

Answer:

_____

c   What is the final cost after the discount?

Answer:

_____

QUESTION 6

The following items are purchased for a holiday play scheme: one box of disposable gloves costing £18, 12 bottles of pure water for £36, toilet rolls for £8.99, paints and brushes for £72 and six hand towels for £49.

a What is the total?

Answer:

_____

b What would be a 10% discount?

Answer:

_____

c What is the final cost after the discount?

Answer:

_____

QUESTION 7

A book company is offering '20% off' the price of any children's books as long as the centre spends at least £100. A family day care centre spends £105 in total.

a How much would the discount be?

Answer:

_____

b How much is the final price?

Answer:

_____

QUESTION 8

A particular range of toddler's nappies are discounted by 15%. If the total price before the discount comes to £245.50 for the nappies, what will the discounted price be?

Answer:

_____

QUESTION 9

A large pack of glitter pens are selling for £16.90 as the recommended retail price. The store has a '20% off 'sale on this item.

a How much will the glitter pens cost during the sale?

Answer:

_____

b How much will be saved by buying the pens at the sale?

Answer:

_____

QUESTION 10

A group of 120 children participate in an excursion to an aquatic centre. The aquatic centre gives the group a 25% discount for each child.

a If the cost per person is £8.00 to go to the aquatic centre, how much will be saved per child?

Answer:

_____

b How much will be saved for the whole group due to the discount?

Answer:

_____

Short-answer questions

Specific instructions to students

- This unit is designed to help you to improve your skills and increase your speed in converting one measurement into another.
- Read the following questions and answer all of them in the spaces provided.
- You need to show all working, you can use the blank Notes pages at the back of this book.

QUESTION 1

How many millimetres are there in 1 cm?

Answer:

QUESTION 2

How many centimetres are there in 1 m?

Answer:

QUESTION 3

How many millimetres are there in 1 m?

Answer:

QUESTION 4

If a child draws two vertical lines every 2 cm for a maths activity, how many vertical lines would be drawn in 10 cm?

Answer:

QUESTION 5

How many millilitres are there in a 1.5 litre bottle of sun cream?

Answer:

QUESTION 6

How many litres are there in 3500 ml of milk?

Answer:

QUESTION 7

A set of outdoor play equipment weighs a quarter of a tonne. How many kilograms is that?

Answer:

QUESTION 8

A delivery truck that delivers play equipment weighs 2 t. How many kilograms is that?

Answer:

QUESTION 9

A toy delivery truck weighs 4750 kg. How many tonnes is that?

Answer:

QUESTION 10

An outdoor play area measures 4.8 m wide and 12 m long. Fencing needs to be placed around this area for the safety and protection of the children. How far is it around the **perimeter** of the play area?

Answer:

TIP

From time to time, you may need to convert inches to centimetres.

Remember: 1 inch = 2.54 cm (you can round this down to 2.5 cm if you wish)

QUESTION 11

While exploring a unit on 'Slithering snakes', each child designed and made a paper snake. Each snake measured 25 cm. What would be the equivalent length of the paper snake in inches?

Answer:

QUESTION 12

A mobile that was based on an Easter theme was hung from the ceiling. If the mobile measured 50 cm, what length would this be equal to in inches?

Answer:

QUESTION 13

Three toddlers made a wooden train that measured 75 cm. What is the equivalent length in inches?

Answer:

QUESTION 14

A team leader noticed that a nut on one of the wheels of a child's bike was loose. A socket was used to tighten it up. The socket measured 25 mm. What is the equivalent size of the socket in inches?

Answer:

QUESTION 15

During a measuring activity for a Maths unit, the children measured the perimeter of a play mat on the floor. If the perimeter is 250 cm, what is the equivalent distance in inches?

Answer:

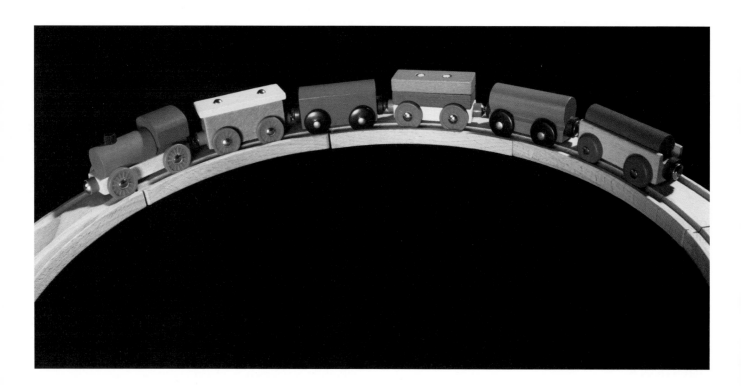

Short-answer questions

Specific instructions to students

- This unit will help you to calculate how much a job is worth and how long you need to complete the job.
- Read the following questions and answer all of them in the spaces provided.
- You need to show all working, you can use the blank Notes pages at the back of this book.

QUESTION 1

Alison works part-time at a nursery and earns £260.60 net (take home) per week. How much does Alison earn per year? (Remember, there are 52 weeks a year.)

Answer

QUESTION 2

Laura starts work at 8.00 a.m. and has a break at 10.30 a.m. for 20 minutes. Lunch starts at 12.30 p.m. and finishes at 1.30 p.m. Laura then works through to 4.00 p.m.

a   How long are the breaks in total?

Answer:

b   How many hours have been worked in total, excluding breaks?

Answer

QUESTION 3

A childcare centre manager gets paid £18.50 per hour and works a 38-hour week. How much are her gross earnings (before tax)?

Answer

QUESTION 4

A **carer** gets paid £513 net for the week's work. From this, she buys new clothes at a cost of £46.90, jewellery worth £49.50, CDs worth £59.97 and a bus ticket which costs £12.60. She also spends £55 on entertainment.

a   What is the total of all money spent?

Answer:

b   How much is left of the week's wage?

Answer

QUESTION 5

The following time is taken by the carers on these activities before lunch with the toddler's and preschooler's group: set up and have breakfast with the children – 45 minutes; choice of play – 60 minutes; morning tea – 30 minutes; painting and craft – 45 minutes; children getting ready for a nap and carers setting up the beds and putting on clean sheets – 25 minutes. How much time, in minutes and hours, has been taken on these activities in total?

Answer:

QUESTION 6

A group from a holiday play scheme leaves the centre at 9.00 a.m. and travels by bus to a recreation park. They arrive at the park at 9.50 a.m. Once the group has been admitted, they have 2 hours to play. Lunch is at 12 noon for 45 minutes. This is followed by structured activities in the main park area, which includes an orientation and safety talk. These activities conclude at 2.00 p.m. Everyone boards the bus and arrives back at the centre at 3.10 p.m.

a   How much time is spent travelling?

Answer:

b   How much time is spent at the park?

Answer:

QUESTION 7

At a family centre, a carer plans a dance activity based on Australian folk dancing. A music CD with eight tracks is put on and the carer wants to finish the activity before the special guest arrives. The eight tracks play for 2 min, 2 min 15 sec, 2 min 45 sec, 3 min, 2 min 35 sec, 1 min 50 sec, 3 min and 15 sec and 3 min and 50 sec.

a   If the CD is put on at 10.00 a.m., what time will it be finished?

Answer:

---

b   The special guest is due to arrive at 11.00 a.m. How much time is left for a break?

Answer:

QUESTION 8

A carer reads several books about wild animals to the preschoolers. This takes 25 minutes. Once completed, the children are asked to draw and colour their two favourite animals, which takes 35 minutes. The drawings are then cut out and stuck on A3 paper to be put up as posters, which takes 25 minutes. Clean-up needs to be done to complete the activity and this takes 12 minutes.

a   How much time, in minutes, has been taken in total?

Answer:

---

b   How much time, in hours and minutes, has been taken in total?

Answer:

QUESTION 9

A manager of a child care centre begins work at 7.00 a.m. and works until 4.00 p.m. There is a morning break for 20 minutes, a lunch break for 60 minutes and an afternoon break of 20 minutes.

a   How much time has been spent on breaks?

Answer:

---

b   How much time has been spent working?

Answer:

QUESTION 10

As part of the daily routine, the following activities are undertaken in the toddlers' room: children remain on their beds once they wake after lunch and are given a book to read for 20 minutes. The toddlers then have quiet activities at their tables which last for 20 minutes. All toddlers then move to the main room for indoor play activities which last 60 minutes. Toddlers are then prepared for outdoor activities, and these take 90 minutes. Next, the toddlers have their choice of programmed play for 45 minutes. This is followed by afternoon tea.

a How much time has been spent on activities in minutes and hours?

Answer:

_____

b How much time has been spent on activities in minutes?

Answer:

_____

QUESTION 11

While working in a nursery, your manager has asked you as part of your Continuing Professional Development to learn how to calculate the staff wages.

The following calculation formulae will be needed in order for you to complete tables 1 and 2.

Taxable amount @ 20% = Gross income – Tax free allowance
Tax payable = (Taxable amount @20%) × 20 ÷ 100
Net income = Gross income – Tax payable
Weekly net income = Net income ÷ 52

a Complete tables 1 and 2 working out the take-home pay for a level 2 qualified nursery nurse and a nursery manager before National Insurance (N.I.) is deducted.

Table 1: level 2 nursery nurse

Gross income per annum	Tax free allowance	Taxable amount @ 20%	Tax payable	Net income	Weekly net income
£12 000	£8105				

Table 2: nursery manager

Gross income per annum	Tax free allowance	Taxable amount @ 20%	Tax payable	Net income	Weekly net income
£25 000	£8105				

b You must now calculate the net income for a level 3 nursery nurse and a manager after tax and National Insurance.

The following calculation formulae will be needed in order to complete tables 3 and 4:

Amount liable for National Insurance (N.I.) = Gross income – allowance before N.I.
National Insurance (N.I.) payable = Amount liable for N.I. × 12 ÷ 100
Annual net income = Gross income – Tax payable – National Insurance payable

Table 3: level 3 nursery nurse

Gross income	Tax free allowance	Taxable amount @ 20%	Tax payable	Allowance before N.I.	Amount liable for N.I. (12%)	N.I. payable	Annual net income
£17 000	£8105		£1779	£7592			

Table 4: nursery manager

Gross income	Tax free allowance	Taxable amount @ 20%	Tax payable	Allowance before N.I.	Amount liable for N.I. (12%)	N.I. payable	Annual net income
£25 000	£8105			£7592			

c   The receptionist/administrator earns £6 per hour and works 40 hours per week. Calculate their yearly income and fill in table 5.

Yearly income:

Table 5: receptionist/administrator

Gross income	Tax free allowance	Taxable amount @ 20%	Tax payable	Allowance before N.I.	Amount liable for N.I. (12%)	N.I. payable	Annual net income
	£8105			£7592			

d   The cook earns £10 per hour for a 35 hour week plus 5 hours overtime at 'time and a half' rate. Work out their yearly income and fill in table 6.

Yearly income:

Table 6: cook

Gross income	Tax free allowance	Taxable amount @ 20%	Tax payable	Allowance before N.I.	Amount liable for N.I. (12%)	N.I. payable	Annual net income
	£8105			£7592			

Unit 14: Squaring Numbers

Section A: Introducing square numbers

Any number squared is multiplied by itself.

EXAMPLE

4 squared $= 4^2 = 4 \times 4 = 16$

QUESTION 1

$6^2 =$

Answer:

QUESTION 2

$8^2 =$

Answer:

QUESTION 3

$12^2 =$

Answer:

QUESTION 4

$3^2 =$

Answer:

QUESTION 5

$7^2 =$

Answer:

QUESTION 6

$11^2 =$

Answer:

QUESTION 7

$10^2 =$

Answer:

QUESTION 8

$9^2 =$

Answer:

QUESTION 9

$2^2 =$

Answer:

QUESTION 10

$4^2 =$

Answer:

Section B: Applying square numbers in the profession (L1) (L2)

Worded practical problems

Specific instructions to students

- This section is designed to help you to improve your skills and increase your speed in calculating **volumes** of rectangular or square objects. The worded questions make the content relevant to everyday situations.
- Read the following questions and answer all of them in the spaces provided.
- You need to show all working, you can use the blank Notes pages at the back of this book.

QUESTION 1

If there are 5×5 crayons in a box, how many crayons are there in total?

Answer:

QUESTION 2

A box of bottled water arrives at an after-school club stacked 6×6. What is the total number of bottles of water?

Answer:

QUESTION 3

There are 12×12 paint brushes packed into a box. How many are in the box?

Answer:

QUESTION 4

An outdoor activity area measures 15 m $\times$ 15 m. How much area is this in square metres for the children to play on?

Answer:

QUESTION 5

A carer draws rows of 8×8 beach balls on a whiteboard. How many beach balls are there?

Answer:

QUESTION 6

A pre-school supervisor unpacks two boxes of hand sanitizer for the toilets. Both boxes contain 4×4 rows of hand sanitizer. How many bottles of hand sanitizer are there in total?

Answer:

QUESTION 7

Three boxes of pots of paint are delivered to a nursery. If the pots are packed in a 6×6 formation in each box, how many pots are there in total?

Answer:

QUESTION 8

A cook stocks the following items in the kitchen: 5×5 sauce bottles, 3×3 packets of crackers and 6×6 bottles of juice. How many items of stock are there in total?

Answer:

QUESTION 9

An outdoor play area has three different areas for children of different ages. The first area for babies measures 4 m × 4 m, the second area for toddlers measures 6 m × 6 m, and the third area for preschoolers measures 11 m × 11 m. How much outdoor play area is available in total?

Answer:

QUESTION 10

A family day care centre has three indoor rooms and two outdoor areas available for children. The indoor rooms measure 3 m × 3 m, 2.5 m × 2.5 m and 4 m × 4 m respectively. The outdoor areas measure at 5 m × 5 m and 3 m × 3 m respectively. How much area is there in total for all areas?

Answer:

Short-answer questions

Specific instructions to students

- This section is designed to help you improve your skills in calculating and simplifying ratios.
- Read the following questions and answer all of them in the spaces provided.
- You need to show all working, you can use the blank Notes pages at the back of this book.

QUESTION 1

If the ratio of carers to children over five years old is 1:8 and there are 48 children over five years old at a day care centre, how many carers are needed?

Answer:

QUESTION 2

If the ratio of carers to children, from the above question, changed to 1 : 12, how many carers are now needed?

Answer:

QUESTION 3

A holiday play scheme has 90 children over five years of age.

a   How many carers are needed if a ratio of 1 : 15 is required?

Answer:

_____

b   If the ratio changes to 1 : 12, does the number of carers need to change? If so, to how many?

Answer:

_____

QUESTION 4

In the babies' room at a nursery, the ratio of carers to babies is 1 : 3. If there are 12 babies in the room, how many carers are needed?

Answer:

_____

QUESTION 5

On an excursion to the beach, the ratio of carers to children is at least one carer to 10 children. If there are 125 children, how many carers will be required?

Answer:

_____

QUESTION 6

If the ratio of carers to children is 1 : 12 and there are 100 children at an out-of-hours care centre, how many carers will need to be present?

Answer:

_____

QUESTION 7

If there are three carers in a babies' room and the ratio of carers to babies is 1 : 3, how many babies would there be?

Answer:

_____

QUESTION 8

The ratio of carers to toddlers decreased from 1 : 15 to 1 : 10 and there are 30 toddlers in the toddler room.

a   How many carers would be needed before the change in ratio?

Answer:

_____

b   How many after?

Answer:

_____

QUESTION 9

A busy childcare centre accommodates 11 babies under three years old. If the ratio of carers to babies is 1 : 3, how many carers will be present?

Answer:

_____

QUESTION 10

A group of 85 children in holiday care gather for a trip to an art-and-craft fair. Normally, the ratio of carers to children would need to be 1 : 15 but on an excursion it changes to 1 : 10. How many more carers are needed for the trip?

Answer:

_____

Unit 16: Rebates L2

Short-answer questions

Specific instructions to students

- This unit will help you to calculate rebates.
- Read the following questions and answer all of them in the spaces provided.
- You need to show all working, you can use the blank Notes pages at the back of this book.

QUESTION 1

A child is in day care for three hours per day for five days a week. The family is charged £77.50 and they receive a rebate of £27.65.

a   How many hours per week has the child been in care?

Answer:

_____

b   How much does the family pay *after* the rebate?

Answer:

_____

QUESTION 2

A family has a child in day care for 12 hours a day for five days. They are charged £310 and they receive a rebate of £110.60.

a   How many hours per week has the child been in care?

Answer:

_____

b   How much does the family pay *after* the rebate?

Answer:

_____

QUESTION 3

Using the information from Question 2, calculate the following if the same child is in day care for four weeks:

a   How many hours would the child have been in care?

Answer:

_____

b   How much will the family be charged *before* the rebate?

Answer:

_____

c   How much will the rebate be?

Answer:

_____

d   How much will the family need to pay *after* the rebate is deducted?

Answer:

_____

QUESTION 4

A child is in day care for 12 hours per day for five days a week. If the weekly cost is £310 and the rebate for the same period is £110.60, how much does it cost to have the child in day care for six months (assume one month = four weeks):

a   before the rebate?

Answer:

_____

b   after the rebate?

Answer:

_____

QUESTION 5

Using the information from Question 4, calculate how much it would cost to have the same child in care for twelve months (52 weeks):

a   before the rebate?

Answer:

_____

b   after the rebate?

Answer:

_____

Unit 17: Reading, Interpreting and Understanding Data L1

Short-answer questions

Specific instructions to students

- The following questions will help you understand and interpret data.
- Read the questions, then answer accordingly.

You have completed your studies in Childcare and are celebrating at home by inviting friends round for a take-away meal. You want to order food for six people in total from the selection available. First you must decide what meals to order for your friends and yourself to eat.

Meal Number	Type of food	Meal feeds	Price of meal
001	vegetarian dishes	one person	£5.40
002	meat dishes	one person	£5.60
003	fish dishes	one person	£5.80
004	vegetarian dishes	two people	£9.20
005	meat dishes	two people	£9.40
006	fish dishes	two people	£9.80
007	vegetarian dishes	three people	£13.60
008	meat dishes	three people	£14.00
009	fish dishes	three people	£14.40
010	vegetarian dishes	four people	£17.40
011	meat dishes	four people	£17.60
012	fish dishes	four people	£18.20

QUESTION 1

List the meal numbers you have chosen, type of food and cost of each selection.

Answer:

_____

QUESTION 2

What is the total cost of the meal for six people? (show your working out)

Answer:

_____

QUESTION 3

The take away offers a 15% discount for telephone orders. How much money will you get off your food order? (show your working)

Answer:

_____

QUESTION 4

What is the total amount payable with the discount applied to your food order? (show your working)

Answer:

_____

QUESTION 5

Draw a table to show your order including the following important information:

- Set meal numbers

- Quantity of each meal ordered

- Price before discount applied

- Amount of discount for each set meal

- Cost of each set meal with discount applied

- Total amount payable

Answer:

QUESTION 6

Your friends agree to share the cost of the food equally. How much will each person pay? (show your working)

Answer:

QUESTION 7

You phone for your meal at 7.00 p.m. and the order should arrive within ¼ of an hour. What time will the food be delivered?

Answer:

QUESTION 8

Double check at least one calculation from those listed above.

Answer:

Types of foods we like! L1

Before you begin, give your answers to these questions:

QUESTION 1

Which foods do you think will be the most popular?

Answer:

QUESTION 2

Which foods do you think will be the least popular?

Answer:

Now ask everyone in your class which foods they like from the list below. Make a tally next to each one.

Which food?	What does it look like?	How many like this?
Burgers		
Piri-piri chicken		
Fish and chips		
Curry		
Pizza		
Hotdogs (frankfurters)		
Fried rice		
Chilli con carne and nachos		
Kebabs		
Sushi		

How were your predictions?

Answer:

_____

_____

_____

TIP

Prediction: to say or estimate what will happen

Turn your tally chart into a pictogram

Try using one ♡ for every two people.

What would half a heart represent?

Answer:

_____

Food type	Pictogram
Burgers	
Piri-piri chicken	
Fish and chips	
Curry	
Pizza	
Hotdogs (frankfurters)	
Fried rice	
Chilli con carne and nachos	
Kebabs	
Sushi	

Now draw a bar chart with your data.

Used squared paper.

It should look something like this (but with different numbers).

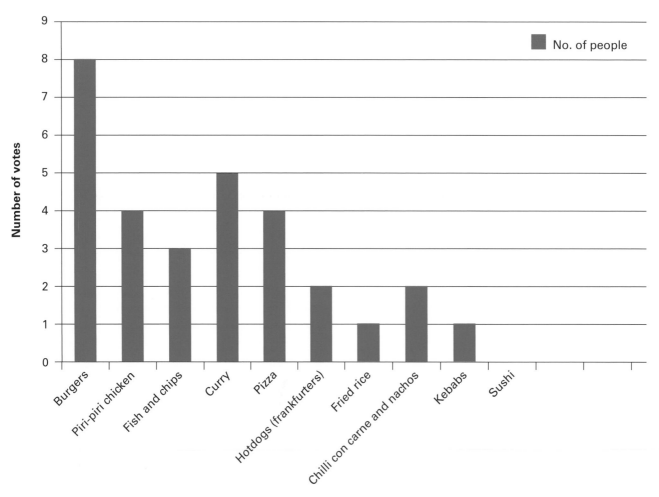

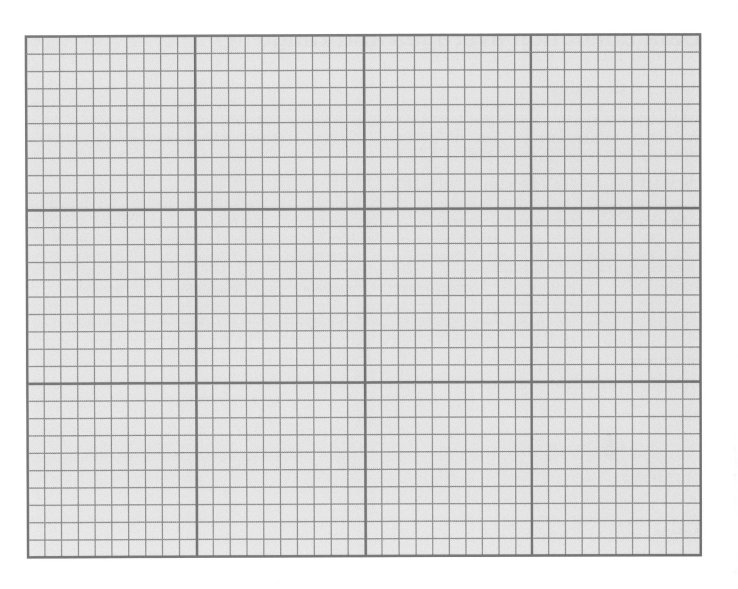

Speaking and listening 🔵

Using your research information on foods we like, you are going to discuss with a partner what food you like and why you like them. What is your experience of the food types shown in the charts?

Make notes of your opinions and any points or questions you may want to ask during your class discussion.

Key questions to consider in your discussion

What did it taste like?

Would you eat that food again?

When did you eat it?

Where did you eat it?

Who did you eat that meal with?

Was it a celebration or everyday meal?

Are there any foods you like from different cultures?

Remember to speak clearly, listen to others and respond appropriately.

Data collection averages and range

Daryl is a nursery manager.

She has been told by a local supermarket that if she spends an average of £500 per month over a 12-month period, then they will give her a reward account card. This rewards cards allows her to have a 2% discount off monthly totals over £500 spend or 5% off spends above £1000.

The table below shows how much Daryl spent in 2012.

January	February	March	April	May	June
£375.89	£417.52	£507.85	£1658.00	£603.57	£512.50
July	**August**	**September**	**October**	**November**	**December**
£500.02	£506.00	£405.78	£510.12	£474.58	£251.59

QUESTION 1

What is the range of Daryl's spending?

Answer:

QUESTION 2

In which month does she spend the least? Why do you think this?

Answer:

QUESTION 3

Does Daryl qualify for a reward account card? Show your working!

Answer:

QUESTION 4

Calculate the savings Daryl could have made each qualifying month if she had been given a reward account card for 2012.

Answer:

What is the **total** amount she could have saved?
(Round your answer to two decimal places.)

Answer:

Unit 18:
Practice Written Exam for the Childcare Profession

Section A: English

Section B: Mathematics

QUESTION and ANSWER BOOK

Section	Topic	Number of questions	Marks
A	English	30	238
B	Mathematics	14	51
		Total 44	Total 289

The sections may be completed in the order of your choice.

Source Document: Job Application (L1)

Read the following source document,
then answer the questions.

VACANCY:

A vacancy has arisen in our nursery for an assistant. The job has a number of key requirements:

Scope of Position

- To work as a member of the nursery team to ensure that all children attending the setting receive high kwality care, Are kept safe and recieve rich and stimulating play experiencis which meet their individuwal needs.

Key Responsibilities

Childcare and Education

- Provide High standards of quality within. the nursery including the enviroment, resources and experiences offered to children.

- Observe, support and extend children's learning.

- Plan appropriately for children using the Early Years Foundation Stage (EYFS) curiculum for guidance.

- Maintain acurate And effective children's records.

- Work in partnership with parents/carers and other famaly members.

- Demonstrate good practice with regard to special needs and inklusion.

- Ensure that children are kept safe And understand, and when necessary follow, Child Protection Procedures.

- Ensure that the nutRitional needs of the children are met and that Food Safety Regulasuns are complied with.

- Comply with the statutory framework for the EYFS and relevant legislation including the Children Act 1989 and 2004.

- Develop and maintain highly profesional working Relationships with advisary teachers schools area SENCOs and other agencies that may visit the setting.

- Learn about current developpments in childcare and education policy and practice.

- Be a key person carrying out all related responsibilaties in building relationnships with a small group of children and their families.

Health and Safety

- Undertake a shared responsibility for health safety and clenliness throughout The nursery.

- Ensure the general cleanliness of the children at all times.

- Adhere to Health and Safety policies, to manage risk and ensure that any remedial action is taken imediately.

- Be fully aware of all emergencay and security procedures e.g. fire precautions security, dropping off and collection of children.

- Operate the highest standard of hygeen and cleanliness in the bedding and nappy changing area and food preparation areas.

Operational

- Promote the nursery to current parents and potential customers.

- Support the manager and staff During inspections by regulatory bodies and to assist in the implementation of any reccomendations.

Staff

- Work as a team with other staff members.

- Support and mentor students.

- Be responsible for participating in all self-development activities including appraisals, supervisions etc.

Communication

- Develop and promote parental partnership and involvement.

General

- Undertake any other duties as reesonably requested by line management.

- Adhere to all nursery policies and procedures.

- Ensure the nursery's Policies on diversity and equal oportunities are adhered to.

Interested applicants must, in the first instance, email the Nursery Manager, mrs Natasha Flowers (natashaflowers@ kidzrus.com) confirming qualifications, experience and availability within ten days of the date of this advert. Interviews will be held within 21 days and any offer of employment is subject to suitable references and data checks.

Questions on Source Document

40 marks

A vacancy as a Nursery Assistant is advertised in the local newspaper and you are interested in applying for that role.

a   Read the source document carefully and correct any spelling mistakes that you may find.   **1 mark per error**

b   There are also a number of punctuation and grammatical errors; locate and correct these.   **1 mark per error**

c   In about 150 words, draft an email to the Manager at KidzRus advising her of your interest in the position. Mention your qualifications, particular skills and qualities along with any experience that you may have.

Answer:

You should make a plan and write a neat copy. Proof read your work and ensure that there are no punctuation or grammatical errors. You may use a dictionary to help with the spelling and definition of words.

Source Document: Childcare Qualifications and Training L2

Read the following source document, then answer the questions.

Caring for children comes naturally to many people, and there are those who are lucky enough to know that childcare is the profession for them. But for some, changing career and building a new vocation in childcare might not be a first consideration.

A variety of skills are necessary in helping children to grow emotionally, physically and socially – so a variety of people with these skills are needed to fulfil these requirements. After all, childcare is a very important aspect of any child's development and well-being, and should be considered as one of the most valuable jobs for creating our future generations.

Childcare is a varied, fun, flexible and ultimately satisfying career path for any person to undertake. The childcare sector is growing fast, and there has never been a better time to enter. The demand for and variety of job opportunities available is remarkably high. So, if you've often wondered whether you could make the switch and change to a career in childcare, you might be surprised at just how easy it could be.

There are many different roles associated with the childcare profession, ranging from managerial roles to hands-on assistant jobs. Of course, if you intend to work in the childcare sector, it's safe to say that you think you're good working with children. But it's best to have an idea of a more specific role, so that you can make the most of your skills and strengths, particularly as working with children requires a lot of dedication, patience and enthusiasm.

Some of the most common positions found in childcare include working within nurseries and schools, within pre-schools and playgroups, private childminding and playwork.

Playwork includes working with children in a capacity that encourages learning and social skills in a fun environment. Out of school clubs and community centres are some of the most common forms of playwork, and can encompass activities such as art and craft, sport, music and drama. If you possess any of these skills, you may find that you're more than suitable in pursuing a career in playwork.

If you intend to work on the business and administration aspect of childcare; you'll need to be organised, and ideally possess a reasonable amount of experience in business supervision or management beforehand. Interpersonal skills will be of paramount importance.

These sorts of skills are transferable from many other professions, but, of course, it helps to have a proven track record that demonstrates you understand the needs of the developing child. This is where training or qualifications might come in handy, or similarly some experience in working in childcare.

When working in childcare, there are certain positions that will need appropriate qualifications to fulfil the requirements of the role. These usually include early years education and care, as well as nursery nurses or team leaders. Working with babies and children with a mental or physical disability may also require specific training, such as psychology or child development (sometimes included as a module within a college course). Also, any first aid training will be a big bonus when working with children.

Studying for a childcare qualification doesn't have to be a full-time undertaking. Although full-time college courses are widespread, there are also many opportunities for would-be mature students to study part-time. Diplomas that can be studied by distance learning from home are an increasingly popular study option for many. A diploma will open up opportunities to train on the job, and receive training for further qualifications, such as NVQ Level 3 or a BTEC.

If you don't currently have the right entry requirements, such as appropriate GCSEs to get yourself onto a college course, you can always try an Access to Higher Education qualification. This is basically a foundation course that will equip you to take your training onto the next step.

There are a few routes to gaining the right qualifications for a career in childcare. Obviously, to a certain degree this can be dependent on the specific position you'd like to undertake. In most cases, there is a college course for each position. You may also be able to train on the job, gaining your qualifications as you learn and take on more responsibility, with regular reviews. For some positions there is the opportunity to combine the two by undertaking a college course while training on the job.

It is hard to define a salary in childcare, as it can depend upon a variety of factors, such as the hours worked and location. Pay scales are determined by location, and tend to be set on a local, rather than national basis. The general rule though, is that the more hours worked, and the more qualifications you have, the higher salary you can expect to receive. To get an idea of local salaries, you can always approach your local Job Centre.

Assessment to Level 2 Source Document

Read the source document and answer the following questions:

QUESTION 1   1 mark

The document provides information about qualifications and training in childcare. Who do you think it is aimed at?

Answer:

_____

_____

_____

_____

_____

QUESTION 2   3 marks

Why is working in childcare important?

Answer:

_____

_____

_____

_____

QUESTION 3   4 marks

List some reasons for working in childcare.

Answer:

_____

_____

_____

_____

QUESTION 4   4 marks

What skills and qualities are required in working in childcare?

Answer:

_____

_____

_____

_____

QUESTION 5   6 marks

Where could you be employed in childcare?

Answer:

_____

_____

_____

_____

QUESTION 6   2 marks

What is meant by 'transferable skills'?

Answer:

_____

_____

_____

_____

QUESTION 7   2 marks

Why would training in working with mental and physical disabilities be important?

Answer:

_____

_____

_____

_____

QUESTION 8   2 marks

Why would training in first aid be useful?

Answer:

_____

_____

_____

_____

QUESTION 9 — 3 marks

What are the training options for somebody without GCSEs?

Answer:

_____

_____

_____

_____

QUESTION 10 — 2 marks

Why would training on the job be useful?

Answer:

_____

_____

_____

_____

QUESTION 11 — 10 marks

Using your dictionary, locate the definitions of the following words:

a   Qualifications

_____

_____

_____

b   Transferable

_____

_____

_____

_____

c   Interpersonal

_____

_____

_____

_____

d   Dedication

_____

_____

_____

_____

e   Foundation

_____

_____

_____

_____

QUESTION 12

You have been asked to draft a personal statement to support your application for a degree course in Early Years Education.

You should include information about your college course, skills and qualities and also particular area of interest that you wish to specialise in. You should also write about why you would be a suitable candidate for study on that particular course and what your career aspirations are.

Use the information provided to write a plan and draft of between 150 and 200 of your own words. You may use a dictionary to help you with spelling and word definitions. Remember to proof read your work to ensure that there are no errors in punctuation or grammar.

Answer:

Job description

Read the following job description then answer the questions.

Job description: Apprentice Nursery Nurse

You will be working in an established nursery. You will have the opportunity to train as a childcare practitioner in a full-time role where you will be performing basic duties to begin.

Your job role will include:

- Reception duties, including meeting and greeting children on their arrival

- Setting out play equipment

- Observing and learning

- Interacting with the children, providing a safe and supportive environment

- Making drinks and snacks for the children

- Attending training as required

Working week

The nursery is open Monday to Friday; therefore you will be required to work these with one day release to college (39 hours per week including training).

Training to be provided

You will receive high levels of support and on the job training. You will be working towards the intermediate Apprenticeship in Childcare (Level 2) and receive on the job training. You will be expected to attend college one day per week where you will receive both theory and practical tuition.

Qualifications required:

Ideally candidates should have GCSE (or equivalent) English and Maths at grade C and above or Key/Functional Skills in English and Maths at level 1. Those candidates who have not achieved the entry level requirements will be required to attend an assessment interview and it will only be on successful completion of the assessment that they will be accepted onto the course. They will also be required to complete Key/Functional Skills at Level 1 as part of their apprenticeship.

Skills required

Good communication skills, able to interact with both staff and service users.

Personal qualities required

Pleasant disposition, as you will be dealing with children and their **primary carers**.

QUESTION 1
1 mark

According to the text, which day is the nursery closed? Tick the correct answer.

(a) Friday	(b) Saturday
(c) Tuesday	(d) Monday

QUESTION 2
3 marks

List three duties that the role will include:

Answer:

_____

_____

_____

QUESTION 3

3 marks

Using a dictionary – explain the word 'communication'

Answer:

_____

_____

QUESTION 4

2 marks

What are the ideal qualifications required?

Answer:

_____

_____

QUESTION 5

1 mark

How many days a week would you be attending college? Tick the correct answer.

(a) Two	(b) Three
(c) One	(d) None

Job application

LITTLE TREASURES CHILDCARE ESTABLISHMENT

We require a Full-time Childcare Practitioner to join our team.

Experience not necessary as we will train you.

If you are looking to enter the childcare profession and have a passion for working with young people, then contact us today!

Write to:

Kerry Brown, Little Treasures Childcare Establishment, 22 Elm Street, Speke, Liverpool LX7 1RD

You have seen this advertisement in your local paper.

You would like to work for this childcare setting as they have a good reputation and they also offer excellent training.

Task

Write a letter of application for this job.

You could include:

- Why you would like to work at this nursery

- Any relevant qualifications

- What experience you have – this could be from other work roles

- What skills and experience you could bring to this job

You should:

- Use correct letter format

- Write in full sentences

- Use correct spelling, punctuation and grammar

Remember to plan your answer before you write your draft and final letter.

Your word count for this activity is a maximum of 275 words.

Answer:

Parents demand more male childcare workers

The Children's Workforce Development Council (CWDC) carried out research in which 55 per cent of parents said they would like a male childcare worker for their nursery-aged children, with two-thirds of single-parent mothers saying they would like a man involved in the care and development of their child.

Early years settings can provide children with access to a male role model. Statistics show that 17 percent of children who live with a single female parent have fewer than two hours a week contact time with a man, while 36 per cent have under six hours. Male early years workers can perform a major role in ensuring these young children have quality contact time with men.

Offering a role model for the boys to look up to was seen as important for 37 per cent of parents, who say that it sets boys a good example, while a quarter believe boys will behave better with a man.

Not only boys stand to benefit. Fifty-seven per cent of parents recognised the fact that men and women have different skills to offer young people, while 52 per cent simply said that an early years setting should better reflect the real gender mix of the world.

Currently there are very few men working in this field. To try to address this dramatic gender imbalance, CWDC is calling on more men to consider a career working in early years.

Thom Crabbe, National Development Manager for Early Years at the Workforce Development Council said:

'Parents are right to want to see more men working in early years. It is important that during the crucial first five years of a child's life they have quality contact with both male and female role models.

'And working with under 5s is definitely a job for the boys. It's one that requires someone who is patient, creative, and bright and one which gives back major rewards. Male workers will get to work in a challenging, stimulating environment with likeminded professionals dedicated to the development of children with positive benefits to babies, toddlers and young children to families and communities.'

Task 1: Comprehension   7 marks

Read the article above then answer the following questions:

QUESTION 1

What percentage of parents say they would like a male childcare worker for their nursery?

Answer:

QUESTION 2

How many children from single-parent female families have fewer than two hours a week contact time with a man?

Answer:

QUESTION 3

How is the CWDC trying to encourage more men to gain employment in early years?

Answer:

_____

_____

_____

QUESTION 4

Who said, 'It is important that during the crucial first five years of a child's life they have quality contact with both male and female role models'.

Answer:

_____

_____

QUESTION 5

Give two reasons why it is important for more men to work in the early years sector.

Answer:

_____

_____

_____

_____

Task 2: Grammar

3 marks

Which of the following are not complete sentences? Tick the complete sentences.

providing someone for the boys to look up to was recognised as important for 37 per cent of parents	
contact with both female and male role models	
CWDC is calling for more men to consider working in early years	
male workers will get to work in a challenging	
two thirds of single-parent mothers say they would like a man involved in the care and development of their young children	
currently there are very few men working in this field	
many early years workers can perform a vital role in ensuring many of these young children have quality contact time	
parents recognised the fact that men and women have different skills	

Task 3: Fact or opinion?

4 marks

Decide which of the following are fact and which are opinion.

There are insufficient numbers of men working in the early years sector.	
Men have the patience to work with children.	
Most parents want to see male employees in their early years settings.	
'Parents are right to want to see more men working in early years'.	
Most children from single parent families do not have enough contact with males.	
Boys need a man to look up to.	
Parents felt it was important to have a gender mix in the nursery to reflect the real world.	
Some children have very little contact with adult males.	

Task 4: Writing

What is your opinion about the topic discussed in the text. Write no less than 200 words to express your point of view. Remember to use the statistics to back up your points and to use quotation marks if you quote any part of the text.

Answer:

Task 5: Speaking and Listening

Using the source document provided, prepare for and contribute to a group discussion, allowing for and responding to others' input. Write out your planned points below. Remember to present your information or point of view clearly and using appropriate language.

Answer:

Section B: Mathematics

Fundraising ⓛ

A nursery is holding a raffle to raise money. You will have to decide how many raffle tickets the nursery expects to sell and what prizes they should buy. Show your working.

QUESTION 1   4 marks

Every year the final number of raffle tickets sold has gone up by about 10%. You think that the number sold will go up by the same percentage this year.

Last year the number of tickets sold was 326.

a   Work out how many more tickets than last year you expect to sell.

Answer:

_____

_____

b   Work out the total number of tickets you expect to sell this year.

Answer:

_____

_____

c   The nursery will sell raffle tickets for £2.50 each. What is the total amount of money from all the tickets you expect to sell?

Answer:

_____

QUESTION 2   2 marks

The nursery only wants you to spend up to a quarter of the money from the tickets on prizes.

Work out the maximum amount of money you can spend on prizes.

Answer:

_____

_____

QUESTION 3   3 marks

You want to buy one expensive first prize and five cheaper prizes. The manager gives you a list of suitable items to choose from.

Suitable items for prizes:	
Trafford Centre Shopping Voucher	£95.00
Digital camera	£91.00
Sat Nav	£38.00
Family Fun Day ticket	£33.00
Watch	£30.00
Chocolate Hamper	£15.00

There must be at least four different items as prizes.

Which items will you buy and what is the total cost?

Answer:

Item	How many of each?	Show your working
	Total Cost_____	

Taking into account the number of raffle tickets you expect to sell, the money the nursery will get from selling that number of raffle tickets, and the cost of the prizes, how much profit will the nursery make?

Check your calculations.

Little Rockers Nursery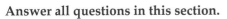

Answer all questions in this section.

Write your answers in the spaces provided.

Megan owns a children's nursery.

The table shows the ages of the 30 children in the nursery.

Name	Age
Nicole	8 months
Molly	2 years 1 month
Andrew	4 years 2 months
Alfie	3 years 3 months
Ellis	2 years 8 months
Lucy	5 months
Ian	4 years 1 month
Sarah	3 years 5 months
Dylan	9 months
Saumya	2 years 9 months
Tyler	2 years 4 months
Ali	3 years 7 months
Baz	14 months
Kudzai	3 years 6 months
Grace	2 years 1 month

Name	Age
Matthew	2 years 8 months
Liberty	18 months
Liam	2 years 1 month
Samantha	3 years 4 months
Raj	12 months
Sophia	4 years 6 months
Ainslee	3 years 9 months
Adele	19 months
Rutha	3 years 4 months
Bobby	3 years 8 months
Damien	2 years 10 months
Ameena	16 months
Robert	3 years 2 months
Henry	4 years
Thomas	3 months

QUESTION 1

3 marks

Megan needs to know how many children are in each of these age groups:

- under 2 years old

- 2 years old

- 3–7 years old.

Design a table or chart to record the number of children in each age group. Complete it for all 30 children in Megan's nursery. Use the box on the following page for your table or chart.

Answer:

QUESTION 2   2 marks

The table below shows the maximum number of children each adult can look after in a nursery.

Age group	Supervision ratio
under 2 years	1 adult for every 3 children
2 years	1 adult for every 4 children
3–7 years	1 adult for every 8 children

Megan would like to have 50 children in the nursery.

She has the following adults for each age group:

under 2 years   5 adults
2 years   4 adults
3–7 years   2 adults

Does Megan have enough adults to look after 50 children? Show your calculations and explain your answer.

Answer:

QUESTION 3   2 marks

How can Megan relocate the adults so she can look after 50 children? Use the box to show your calculations and your answer.

Answer:

QUESTION 4   4 marks

Megan pays her nursery staff £5.95 per hour.

Each person works 8 hours per day Monday to Friday There are 11 nursery staff.

Megan needs to calculate how much she pays her staff in total each week.

Show how she can calculate this.

Answer:

QUESTION 5   5 marks

Little Rockers has a room for the 2-year-old children.

Megan wants to have two separate spaces in the room. One space will be for a quiet area, the other space will be for creative play. Megan draws a plan of the room.

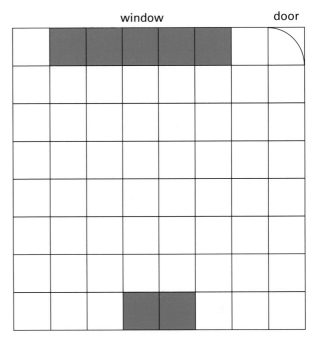

Key: 1 square on the plan = 1 m in the room

The quiet area will be in a corner of the room. It will be in the shape of a rectangle with dimensions 2 m by 3 m.

a Draw the quiet corner on the plan.

The space for creative play will be along a wall. It will be in the shape of a rectangle. It will have an area of 12 m².

b Draw the space for creative play on the plan.

The rest of the room is for active play. Megan thinks she needs at least 20 m² of space for active play.

c Does she have at least 20 m² of space for active play? Show why you think this.

Use the plan above to show your answers.

Spinning Top

Spinning Top is a chain of nurseries that runs an additional service taking and collecting children from a variety of schools.

The chain uses five minibuses to ferry the children.

The minibuses are the same make and model.

The table below gives information about the value and ages of the five minibuses.

New	1 year old	2 years old	3 years old	4 years old	5 years old
£16,000	£11,500	£ 9,800	£ 8,500	£ 7,400	£ 6,500

Spinning Top wants to be able to estimate the value of a minibus using its age.

QUESTION 1   4 marks

Draw a graph Spinning Top could use to estimate the value of a minibus.

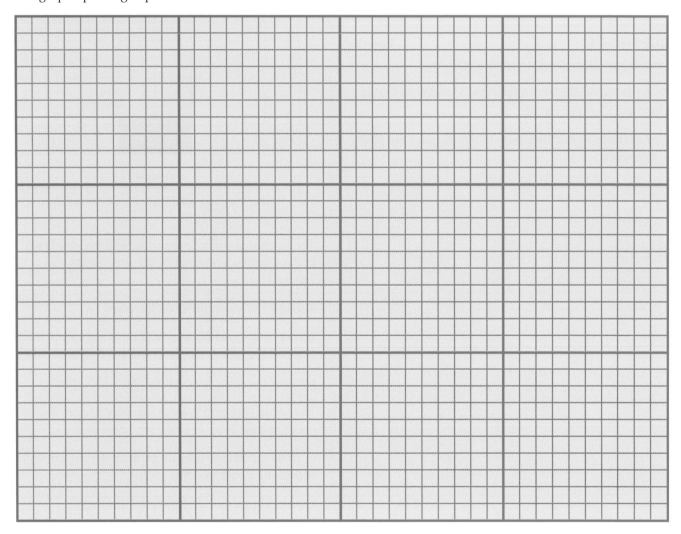

QUESTION 2   2 marks

Spinning Top wants to buy another minibus of the same make and model to take and collect additional children.

One van is 2.5 years old.

How much should the setting expect to pay for the minibus?

Use the box to show clearly how you get your answer.

Answer:

Helping Helen

Helen interviews people for positions on a holiday play scheme. Each person she interviews gives her a claim form for expenses.

Helen checked the claim form and found some errors. She circles all the mistakes on the form.

Claim form		
Complete all sections		
Reason for claim	**Details**	**Total**
Train fare	Return ticket	£122.50
Car travel	28 miles at 27p per mile	£8.16
Travel refreshments	£4.40 £3.80	£7.20
		Total claim £137.36

The cost of car travel is now 29p per mile.

What should the correct total claim be?

Answer:

_____

Use this box to show clearly how you get your answer.

Answer:

QUESTION 2

Helen has to organise five interviews in one day.

- The five people are Redet, Grace, Molly, Matthew and Liberty.

- Each person will have three separate interviews.

- Each person will be interviewed once in each of the three rooms.

- Anyone not being interviewed will wait in the waiting room.

- Each interview will last 15 minutes.

- There are five minutes between each interview.

- The first interviews will start at 9.00 a.m.

- All rooms can be used for interviews at the same time.

Draw a chart or table to show the times and rooms for the five people being interviewed.

Use this box to show your working clearly and draw your chart or table.

Answer:

QUESTION 3

Helen has been asked to compare the pay for four similar jobs advertised in a newspaper.

Kids 4 Us	*Cleveleys Preparatory School*
Nursery nurse	Classroom Support
Pay: £23,000 per year	Full Time: 30 hours per week
	Pay: £15 per hour
Scoundrels for Skool	*Chimney Pots Play Scheme*
Childminder	Play worker
Pay: £18,000 plus additional overtime as required by parents £4,000.	Salary of £20,000 + team bonus of 20% of salary

How much does Cleveleys Preparatory School pay per year?

Answer:

_____

Use this box to show clearly how you get your answer.

Answer:

Which job pays the most money?

Answer:

_____

Use this box to show clearly how you get your answer.

Answer:

Childcare Glossary

After-school club A service providing care to primary school aged children before and / or after the normal school day.

Carer A person who can provide care for someone else's child or children.

Childcare benefit A payment made by the government to families to assist with the overall cost of childcare.

Childcare tax credit A payment made by the government to help eligible working families with the costs associated with childcare.

Childminder A flexible form of childcare where care is provided in an approved childminder's home.

Creche Services that provide short periods of care for children under school age. It can be accessed by families on either a regular or irregular basis. The reasons parents use this type of provision may be due to casual, shift-work or part-time work, shopping, respite care, crisis and emergency care or attending appointments.

Day care centres Settings that usually care for children under school age but may also provide after-school care and holiday care for older children. Examples of people and organizations that may provide day care include private operators, local councils, community organizations, employers and not-for-profit organisations.

Family day care A service referring to a network of experienced carers who can provide care and developmental activities for other people's children.

Holiday play scheme A service providing care to primary school aged children during the school holiday periods only. The operating hours for these centres is generally between 7.00 a.m. and 6.00 p.m. each week day.

Nanny A person who may be employed by a family on either a live-in or live-out basis. A nanny usually undertakes all tasks related to the care of a child or children. The types of duties that a nanny may provide are generally restricted to childcare and the domestic tasks related to childcare.

Non-school child A child who is yet to attend school.

Nursery A profit-making service provided by qualified staff in a setting that provides care and developmental activities.

Parent and Toddler group A service, usually non-profit-making, to provide the opportunity for parents and young children to socialize together.

Playgroup A setting that provides short periods of care for children usually over two years of age and under the school age of five years, providing the opportunity for children to learn through play.

Pre-school A setting that provides short periods of care for children who are nearing school age. Although there is some learning through play, these are more structured and academic.

Primary carer The sole or major provider responsible for ongoing daily care of a child, with the ability to make day-to-day decisions about the child's care, including their welfare and development.

English Glossary

Adjective   A type of word that describes NOUNS (things, people and places), for example *sharp*, *warm* or *handsome*.

Adverb   A type of word that describes VERBS (things happening), for example *slowly*, *often* or *quickly*.

Apostrophe   A PUNCTUATION mark with two main functions: (1) shows where letters have been missed out when words or phrases are shortened, for example changing *cannot* to *can't*, or *I will* to *I'll*; (2) shows where a NOUN 'possesses' something, for example *Dave's bike*, *the cat's whiskers* or *St John's Wood*.

Capital letter   Used to begin a SENTENCE, to begin the names of people, days, months and places, and for abbreviations such as *RSPCA* or *FBI*.

Comma   A PUNCTUATION mark that has many uses, usually to separate phrases in a long SENTENCE so that it is easier to read and understand, or to separate items in a list.

Formal language   The type of language used when speaking to or writing to someone you don't know, such as your bank manager (e.g. 'I am writing to request a bank statement').

Full stop   A PUNCTUATION mark used at the end of SENTENCES.

Future tense   The VERB forms we use to talk about things that will happen in future (e.g. 'I *will watch* television tonight').

Homophone   A word that sounds the same as another word, but has a different spelling and meaning, for example *break* and *brake*.

Informal language   The type of language used when you are speaking to or writing to someone you know well, such as a friend (e.g. 'Hi, how are you? Do you fancy coming to the cinema with me?').

Instructions   A series or list of statements designed to show someone how to do something, for example to use some equipment or to follow some rules.

Noun   A word used to refer to a thing, person or place, for example *chair*, *George* or *Sheffield*.

Paragraph   A section of writing about the same subject or topic, that begins on a new line and consists of one or more SENTENCES.

Past tense   The VERB forms we use to talk about things that have happened in the past (e.g. 'I *watched* television last night').

Present tense   The VERB forms we use to talk about things that are happening now (e.g. 'I *am watching* television').

Pronouns   Words that are used instead of NOUNS (things, people and places), for example *he*, *she*, *we*, *it*, *who*, *something*, *ourselves*.

Punctuation   Marks used in writing to help make it clear and organized, by separating or joining together words or phrases, or by adding or changing emphasis.

Question mark   A PUNCTUATION mark used at the end of a question, to show that you have asked something.

Sentence   A group of words, beginning with a CAPITAL LETTER and ending with a FULL STOP, QUESTION MARK or exclamation mark, put together using correct grammar, to make a meaningful statement or question, etc.

Verb   Word used to indicate an action, for example *mix*, *smile* or *walk*.

Mathematics Glossary

Actual   The exact calculation of a set of numbers.

Analogue clock   A clock that displays minute and hour hands and shows the time changing continuously.

Area   The size of a surface; the amount of space in a two-dimensional shape or property, e.g. the floor space of a room or flat.

Decimal   A way of organizing numbers based around the number ten (the most familiar system used in the world today).

Decimal point   A mark, often a full stop, used in a number to divide between whole numbers and FRACTIONS of whole numbers shown in DECIMAL form.

Digital clock   A clock that tells the time using numbers instead of hands and shows the time changing digitally – from one exact value to the next.

Estimate   (1) A calculation that requires a rough guess rather than working out the actual figure; (2) to work out this value.

Fraction   A quantity or amount that is not a whole number, e.g. less than 1. A part of a whole number.

Imperial   The British system of units for weights and measures before the METRIC system, including pounds, stones, miles, feet and inches.

Mean   A form of average of a set of numbers. To calculate the mean, add all of the numbers together and then divide by how many numbers there are.

Median   A form of average of a set of numbers. To calculate the median, place the numbers in numerical order and then find the middle number.

Metric   An international DECIMAL system of units for weights and measures, including kilograms, grams, kilometres, metres and centimetres.

Mode   A form of average of a set of numbers. To calculate the mode, look for the number that appears most often.

Percentage   A proportion, or FRACTION, that means part of one hundred.

Perimeter   The total lengths of all of the sides of a two-dimensional shape or AREA, e.g. the distance around the outside of a room.

Range   The difference between the largest and smallest numbers in a set of figures.

Ratio   A way to compare the amounts of things – how much of one thing there is compared to how much of another thing.

Scales   An instrument used to measure the weight of an object or person.

Volume   The amount of three-dimensional space that an object occupies.

Formulae and Data

Circumference of a Circle

$C = \pi \times d$
where: C = circumference, π = 3.14, d = diameter

Diameter of a Circle

$d = \frac{C}{\pi}$
Where: C = circumference, π = 3.14, d = diameter

Area

$A = l \times b$

Area = length × breadth and is given in square units

Volume of a Cube

$V = l \times w \times h$

Volume = length × width × height and is given in cubic units

Volume of a Cylinder

$V_c = \pi \times r^2 \times h$

Where: V_c = volume of a cylinder, π = 3.14, r = radius, h = height

Times Tables

1
1 × 1 = 1
2 × 1 = 2
3 × 1 = 3
4 × 1 = 4
5 × 1 = 5
6 × 1 = 6
7 × 1 = 7
8 × 1 = 8
9 × 1 = 9
10 × 1 = 10
11 × 1 = 11
12 × 1 = 12

2
1 × 2 = 2
2 × 2 = 4
3 × 2 = 6
4 × 2 = 8
5 × 2 = 10
6 × 2 = 12
7 × 2 = 14
8 × 2 = 16
9 × 2 = 18
10 × 2 = 20
11 × 2 = 22
12 × 2 = 24

3
1 × 3 = 3
2 × 3 = 6
3 × 3 = 9
4 × 3 = 12
5 × 3 = 15
6 × 3 = 18
7 × 3 = 21
8 × 3 = 24
9 × 3 = 27
10 × 3 = 30
11 × 3 = 33
12 × 3 = 36

4
1 × 4 = 4
2 × 4 = 8
3 × 4 = 12
4 × 4 = 16
5 × 4 = 20
6 × 4 = 24
7 × 4 = 28
8 × 4 = 32
9 × 4 = 36
10 × 4 = 40
11 × 4 = 44
12 × 4 = 48

5
1 × 5 = 5
2 × 5 = 10
3 × 5 = 15
4 × 5 = 20
5 × 5 = 25
6 × 5 = 30
7 × 5 = 35
8 × 5 = 40
9 × 5 = 45
10 × 5 = 50
11 × 5 = 55
12 × 5 = 60

6
1 × 6 = 6
2 × 6 = 12
3 × 6 = 18
4 × 6 = 24
5 × 6 = 30
6 × 6 = 36
7 × 6 = 42
8 × 6 = 48
9 × 6 = 54
10 × 6 = 60
11 × 6 = 66
12 × 6 = 72

7
1 × 7 = 7
2 × 7 = 14
3 × 7 = 21
4 × 7 = 28
5 × 7 = 35
6 × 7 = 42
7 × 7 = 49
8 × 7 = 56
9 × 7 = 63
10 × 7 = 70
11 × 7 = 77
12 × 7 = 84

8
1 × 8 = 8
2 × 8 = 16
3 × 8 = 24
4 × 8 = 32
5 × 8 = 40
6 × 8 = 48
7 × 8 = 56
8 × 8 = 64
9 × 8 = 72
10 × 8 = 80
11 × 8 = 88
12 × 8 = 96

9
1 × 9 = 9
2 × 9 = 18
3 × 9 = 27
4 × 9 = 36
5 × 9 = 45
6 × 9 = 54
7 × 9 = 63
8 × 9 = 72
9 × 9 = 81
10 × 9 = 90
11 × 9 = 99
12 × 9 = 108

10
1 × 10 = 10
2 × 10 = 20
3 × 10 = 30
4 × 10 = 40
5 × 10 = 50
6 × 10 = 60
7 × 10 = 70
8 × 10 = 80
9 × 10 = 90
10 × 10 = 100
11 × 10 = 110
12 × 10 = 120

11
1 × 11 = 11
2 × 11 = 22
3 × 11 = 33
4 × 11 = 44
5 × 11 = 55
6 × 11 = 66
7 × 11 = 77
8 × 11 = 88
9 × 11 = 99
10 × 11 = 110
11 × 11 = 121
12 × 11 = 132

12
1 × 12 = 12
2 × 12 = 24
3 × 12 = 36
4 × 12 = 48
5 × 12 = 60
6 × 12 = 72
7 × 12 = 84
8 × 12 = 96
9 × 12 = 108
10 × 12 = 120
11 × 12 = 132
12 × 12 = 144

Multiplication Grid

	1	2	3	4	5	6	7	8	9	10	11	12
1	1	2	3	4	5	6	7	8	9	10	11	12
2	2	4	6	8	10	12	14	16	18	20	22	24
3	3	6	9	12	15	18	21	24	27	30	33	36
4	4	8	12	16	20	24	28	32	36	40	44	48
5	5	10	15	20	25	30	35	40	45	50	55	60
6	6	12	18	24	30	36	42	48	54	60	66	72
7	7	14	21	28	35	42	49	56	63	70	77	84
8	8	16	24	32	40	48	56	64	72	80	88	96
9	9	18	27	36	45	54	63	72	81	90	99	108
10	10	20	30	40	50	60	70	80	90	100	110	120
11	11	22	33	44	55	66	77	88	99	110	121	132
12	12	24	36	48	60	72	84	96	108	120	132	144

Maths and English for Childcare
Online Answer Guide

To access the Answer Guide for Maths and English for Childcare follow these simple steps:

1) Copy the following link into your web browser:

http://www.cengagebrain.co.uk/shop/isbn/9781408083123

2) Click on the Free Study Tools Link.

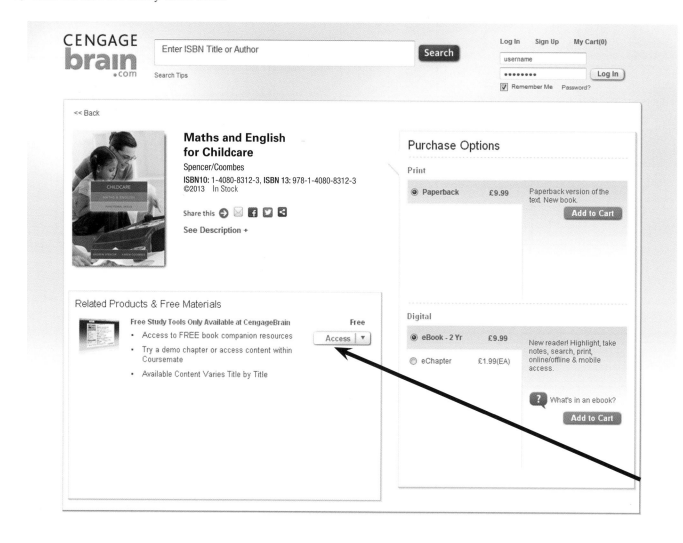

Notes

Notes